RETIREMENT

APPROVED

RETIREMENT APPROVED
Your Guide to a Secure and Successful Retirement

ISBN: 978-1-964046-19-8

Expert
Press
www.ExpertPress.net

Copyediting by Wendy Lukasiewicz
Proofreading by Heather Dubnick
Text design and composition by Emily Fritz
Cover design by Casey Fritz

RETIREMENT (APPROVED)

Your Guide to a Secure and Successful Retirement

Steven Paul, CFP®
Matt Paul, CFP®

We'd like to dedicate this book

To our parents

For giving us the belief that anything was attainable if you were willing to work for it, for instilling the values that we now pass on to our own children, and for being there every step of the way.

To our wives

For always offering nothing but encouraging words and unwavering support through the tough times and long nights. Words cannot express how much we appreciate and love you.

CONTENTS

A Note from the Authors

Any words or phrases set in **bold** will be
defined in the glossary in the back of this book.

Please be aware that you should consult with
a financial professional prior to implementing
any strategies discussed in this book. All case
studies are hypothetical and used to explain
retirement strategies in a relatable way.

We sincerely hope this book helps prepare you
for your retirement journey.

Cheers to your future retirement!

Introduction

The best investment you can make, is an investment in yourself. The more you learn, the more you'll earn.

– Warren Buffett

Congratulations!

If you're reading this book, you're taking your first step toward a successful retirement. After working for decades to provide for your family and loved ones, this is *your* time. Your time to travel, to spoil your grandchildren, to bask all day in the sun around the pool, to achieve whatever goals you have for retirement. You've saved your whole life, you have a reliable Social Security check, and if you're lucky, you may even have a pension. Your children are doing well. Maybe they still need help financially from time to time, but for the most part, they're making their way. Your retirement years, you think, could be the best years of your life.

Trouble is, you're not sure how to get the most out of your money and your retirement. The thought of retiring might make you nervous. You may be second guessing yourself, and you may become fearful to give up the career you've worked so long to master. You may start to wonder what the heck you're going to do all day, or you might even question if you've saved enough money. In your retirement years, the last thing you want to do is be a burden on your children. Ideally, you would like to leave them a healthy inheritance.

Retirement and the years leading up to it can undoubtably be a stressful time. What is meant to be a time of joy and relaxation can quickly turn to stress and anxiety as you enter the next phase of your life.

Take a deep breath. As financial planners who specialize in retirement planning, we see this all the time. Our clients tend to do a great job of setting themselves up for retirement, but once they near the finish line, doubt starts to creep in. This is why having a plan is critical. When you have a retirement plan, it helps to alleviate any fear and anxiety about the financial aspect of retirement. The lifestyle side, well, that's another story.

Think about what you envision for your retirement, and ask yourself the following questions:

- What do you want to do in retirement?
- Who do you want to spend time with?
- Do you want to learn any new skills?
- Do you want to still work?
- Where would you like to travel?
- What would make you feel fulfilled?

If you struggled to answer these questions, you're not alone. After working with retirees for over a decade, we started to notice a pattern with their answers. We used our wonderful clients as inspiration to turn that pattern into a list of twelve retirement personalities. This is all in good fun, and you may find that you fit into multiple categories or maybe even into a category of your own. Read through the retirement personalities and pick what matches you best.

The "One More Year" Retiree

The "one more year" retiree is always one year away from retirement. They say they're one year away, but then a year from now they'll say they're one year away again!

You may fall into this category if you love your job. Sometimes, this type of retiree doesn't want to hang it up, which generally makes planning for their retirement easier because it gives their accounts more time to grow.

The "Retire Yesterday" Retiree

The "retire yesterday" retiree is the exact opposite of the "one more year" retiree. This retiree wants to see a plan, crunch the numbers with an advisor, and pull the trigger on retirement.

The "Travel the World" Retiree

As you probably guessed, the "travel the world" retiree wants to get in as many vacations in as possible. After all, you were working all those years and always wanted to travel to Europe, or Alaska, or anywhere the world takes you.

This lifestyle requires what we call a "frontloaded retirement plan." If you're retiring at sixty-five, maybe we plan for an additional $10,000 to $20,000 per year to help fund vacations and travel. We'll have that fall off or reduce in your mid-to late seventies once you've gotten your travel goals in and begin to slow down.

The "Now That I See the Plan" Retiree

The "now that I see the plan" retiree plans to retire in three to five years. But once we begin planning, they see what their portfolio can generate, and they realize they have the potential to retire earlier than they thought. This type of retiree is a favorite to work with. They're some of the happiest people when they get the news they can retire.

The "Back to Work" Retiree

The "back to work" retiree has become a more popular choice these days. There are countless benefits to going back to work. You may opt for a job with a different company, or you could stay with your current company in a lesser role. You may want to work on your own time or work from home in your pajamas.

Some of our clients start entirely new careers or even invent products. Some of our clients pick up a part-time job doing something they enjoy to help with their income needs in their early years of retirement.

The "Busier Than Ever" Retiree

You may not be able to predict if the "busier than ever" retiree will be you, but once you're retired, there's a good chance you'll find yourself saying, "I'm busier than ever." This type of retiree always wonders how they found the time to do routine things when they were working, because it now seems like a full-time job.

The "Family Is Everything" Retiree

The "family is everything" retiree lives for their family. Whether its relocating to be near their children, or spoiling the grandchildren, or spending time with nieces and nephews, brothers or sisters, their ideal retirement is maintaining close relationships with the ones they love.

This could also involve taking care of a parent. People like to lend a helping hand, which is always time well spent, even if exhausting. To these retirees, leaving a legacy to their heirs is typically of high importance.

The "Hobby Becomes My Jobby" Retiree

Do you find yourself dreaming of a little white ball? If you answered yes to that question, you may fall into the "hobby becomes my jobby" category. Golf is a great way to stay active in retirement, both physically and mentally. But . . . it can also drive you mad.

The "Big Spender" Retiree

As the name suggests, the "big spender" retiree wants to spend the big bucks. Believe it or not, this type of retiree is quite rare. Most retirees aren't looking to spend their hard-earned nest egg on expensive cars or homes. A detailed budget is critical for this retiree.

The "RV" Retiree

We've had numerous clients embrace the RV life, and they're in a different state every time we talk to them.

One small problem is that RVs aren't cheap. But this retiree is willing to pay the up-front cost to have the ability to go anywhere, anytime.

The "Quiet Life" Retiree

The "quiet life" retiree looks forward to exiting the workforce and getting off the grid. Here in Michigan, there's a good chance they'll head to a cottage "up north."

If you're in this category, your hobbies might include camping, reading, animals, charity work, fishing, and gardening. As such, "quiet life" retirees typically have a modest budget and have no problem sticking to it.

The "Day Trader" Retiree

The "day trader" retiree lives to buy and sell stocks. Their ideal time is spent enjoying a morning coffee in front of the computer waiting for the opening bell. This retiree is looking for the next hot stock and enjoys talking stocks with their friends.

It's fine to trade stocks as a hobby, but you shouldn't be in front of a computer from 9:30 a.m. to 4:00 p.m. all day every day throughout your retirement.

(ONE)
Retirement Approved

The first step to becoming "retirement approved" is figuring out what you're going to do with your life after work. When you work a certain job for years or even decades, it tends to become your identity. Losing that identity can be a challenge. You must have a vision for what you want out of retirement, and you must figure it out before you retire. We'll talk more about finding happiness in retirement later in this book, but for now pick a few retirement personalities you feel are the most relatable.

Beyond your retirement personality, you need to understand what retirement is and the unique challenges your generation is facing.

Unsurprisingly, most retirees have no idea how to best use their assets to support a three-to-four-decade retirement. When you look at retirements of previous generations, it seems like it was much simpler . . . because it was. A basic mix of **stocks, bonds,** and **certificates of deposit (CDs),** coupled with the greatest economic boom ever recorded in US history, was all most retirees needed. Add in a strong pension to pair with Social Security, not to mention the shorter longevity and lesser health care costs, and you can see why retirement planning wasn't as complicated as it is today.

Retirement Trivia

Retirement hasn't been around forever, so do you know when the concept of retirement was created?

   a. The late 1600s

   b. The early 1700s

   c. The late 1700s

   d. The late 1800s

The answer can be found on page 175.

Looking back one hundred years, on the heels of World War I, much of the modern US financial system we know today began to take form. Electricity was starting to become part of daily life, and radio programs were now becoming mainstream. And most importantly, as innovation was booming, the market was flourishing.

From 1924 to 1929, investing became more accessible to the middle class, while the Dow surged 294.66 percent. **Mutual funds** were first introduced in this era of investing, allowing investors to diversify rather than to hold riskier individual stock. On Tuesday, October 29, 1929, the Dow crashed 13 percent in one day, losing over 30 percent that week. Twenty-five years and two wars later, the Dow finally recovered. By that time, it was too late; retirements for many were nonexistent.

To help protect retirees, President Franklin D. Roosevelt enacted the Social Security Act of 1935. The modern concept of retirement, where individuals stop working and have the financial support to do so, became more widespread with Social Security and the availability of company pension plans in the mid-twentieth century. After the recovery of the Dow from the Great Depression, the market would be stagnant from the mid-1950s to mid-1970s because of the Vietnam War.

New Financial Tools

Over the next few decades, we saw further innovations in the financial industry. **Hedge funds** started in 1949, followed by **private equity, real estate investment trusts**, and **venture capital** (these are alternative investments not normally available to the average investor). The **variable annuity** was created in 1952. In 1976 Jack Bogle created the first **index fund**, followed by the first **exchange-traded fund (ETF)** in 1993. Later in the 1990s **fixed indexed annuities** were invented. Now, over the past decade, we've seen the rise of an entirely new asset class with **cryptocurrencies**.

Suffice to say, we've seen a great deal of innovation in the financial industry with new strategies and vehicles being released much more frequently.

Those working and saving for retirement throughout 2000 to 2020 saw quite the interesting two decades. From

2000 to 2009 we endured two life-changing recessions with the tech bubble and the global financial crisis. Following the global financial crisis we saw over a decade of low interest rates and a booming stock market. And nobody needs a reminder of the recent stock market downturn as a result of the COVID-19 pandemic and subsequent inflation issues.

Retirement used to be simple, but today it's a much more complex planning task. In the past retirees depended on Social Security for more of their income. Pensions helped cover the remainder of their income needs. Enormous global growth powered the stock market. Bonds were stable and had great returns thanks to decreasing **interest rates** over the last thirty-plus years. Even CDs had solid returns. Health care wasn't much of a concern and was likely covered by employers. Life expectancies weren't as long. A simple 60 percent stock / 40 percent bond portfolio could easily get you through retirement, assuming a safe withdrawal rate.

Retiring in the 2020s

The innovation boom we saw in the roaring 20s may look to be repeated a century later, as the 2020s have brought us the rise of artificial intelligence. The pace of technological progress is accelerating exponentially. No longer confined to our smartphones or online shopping experiences, technology now underpins virtually every aspect of our lives, including the way we conduct business and make investment decisions. It forms the fundamental infrastructure of every industry and enterprise, shaping the very foundation of our modern society and economy.

However, retirees are facing many new challenges amidst the current economic landscape. Social Security is underfunded and likely won't keep up with true inflation. Pensions are few and far between. Global growth has slowed, making the equity markets less dependable. The thirty-year bond bull market has likely ended, as we saw a generational crash in the bond market in 2022. Health care costs have skyrocketed. We're living much longer, as the Society of Actuaries states that a healthy male at retirement age sixty-five can expect to live to eighty-eight, and a healthy female to ninety.[1] And to top it all off, newer strategies like index funds, **alternatives**, and annuities have left retirees as confused as ever as to what they should be doing with their money.

There are new questions we need answers to:

- How should my portfolio be allocated to meet my retirement goals?
- How much income can my portfolio generate in a safe way?
- What is inflation going to do to my expenses, and how am I going to keep up with it throughout a potential thirty-year retirement?
- What can I expect from Social Security?

---

1   Kate Beattie, "Longevity: Don't Plan for an Average Retirement," *Capital Ideas*, October 26, 2023, https://www.capitalgroup.com/advisor/insights/articles/ir-retirement-longevity.html.

- If there's a market downturn, how will I generate income in retirement?
- If my spouse passes away, how will that affect my retirement?
- If I experience a long-term care event, how will I pay for that?

There are so many more questions that we need answered when planning for retirement. Retiring in today's world can be complex and is vastly different than the retirements of previous generations.

Retirement has evolved substantially over the last century. Heck, it's changed dramatically since your parents' retirement. Because of this, retirement planning has become a well-defined niche in the financial planning industry.

It's critical that retirees find an advisor who will invest in their lives and their future goals, and who will help answer these new questions retirees are asking themselves. No one wants to outlive their money and become a burden to their families. Beyond that, our retirement goals differ tremendously. It all depends on the person. Some want to travel the world. Some want to live the simple life and leave some money behind for their family. Others have entirely different goals, pensions, and portfolios.

The typical retiree lacks the expertise to design and maintain a portfolio that allows them to live out secure, comfortable, and rewarding nonworking lives, regardless of how well they set themselves up for their retirement years.

Case Study

John and Jennifer retired earlier this year. They believe they have everything covered, but after losing nearly 40 percent of their retirement portfolio in the 2008 financial crisis, they want to make sure. In many ways, they're in an excellent position.

Both started Social Security at roughly $1,750 per month, both have pensions of roughly $1,500 per month, and their portfolio is worth $1 million. With a monthly budget of $9,500, they can cover the majority of their monthly expenses with their pensions and Social Security and still have room in their budget to travel and to hopefully leave an inheritance to their children and grandchildren.

For simplicity purposes, let's assume John and Jennifer need to generate $3,000 per month from their million-dollar portfolio. This represents a withdrawal rate of 3.6 percent, which is under the common **4 percent withdrawal rate** rule of thumb.

Retirement Trivia

For a retiree with $1 million, the 4 percent rule states that a retiree could reasonably expect to take $40,000 out of the portfolio on an annual basis. During a low interest rate environment, what would be considered a safe withdrawal rate?

   a. 1.5 percent
   b. 2.4 percent
   c. 3.0 percent
   d. 3.5 percent

The answer can be found on page 176.

On the surface, John and Jennifer looked like they were sitting pretty, but when we dug a little deeper, their retirement picture became less clear.

Like most of us, John and Jennifer have yet to consider the loss of income that accompanies the eventual passing of a spouse. John was sixty-seven years old and already had health issues. If he were to pass, Jennifer would instantly lose some of his pension and his entire Social Security check. With this reduction in income, Jennifer wouldn't be able to cover her expenses and would have to increase withdrawals from the portfolio or alter her lifestyle—the last thing any of us want to do in retirement.

They also haven't thought much about the increased health care expenses that come with getting older. A minor health crisis could cause major financial problems for John and Jennifer; a more serious, long-term care event could put them in a precarious financial situation. If they become seriously ill, they would have no room in their budget to pay their medical bills, and they would have to rely on their children for financial assistance or at-home care.

On top of that, the couple's portfolio is extremely risky. Like most of us, their portfolio was designed to get the best possible return while John and Jennifer were working, which meant much of their portfolio is heavily invested in equities. This approach made sense when they were working, and their portfolio's primary objective was growth, but not so much now. They could focus on growth during their working years because they had the advantages of a longer time horizon and didn't need to rely on their portfolio for income. As the market went through its ups and downs, they were earning regular paychecks, which allowed them to stay invested without affecting their lifestyle.

This approach makes sense when you're working; it makes *no* sense when you're approaching retirement or already retired.

John and Jennifer worked long and hard to build a portfolio that would provide them with a secure and comfortable retirement. They didn't work all those years to risk losing their portfolio to the market in retirement. With all the risk built into their portfolio, its value could fall from $1 million to $600,000 if a significant market correction were to occur. This would be devastating to their retirement goals. Their annual safe withdrawal amount would drop in lockstep with their portfolio, which could lead to making some uncomfortable decisions. Do they forgo a few vacations they've always wanted to go on? Maybe they leave less money to their heirs? None of us want to be forced into making these decisions.

Why Sequence of Returns Matters

Let's take a look at how John and Jennifer's retirement would have looked in two different time periods if they were invested in the Standard & Poor's (S&P) 500.

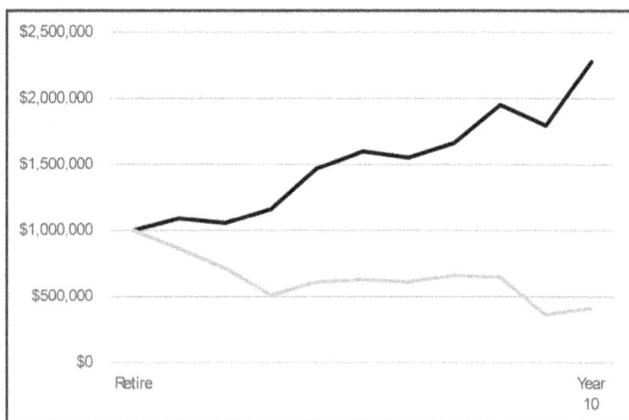

The top line is if they were to retire in 2010, versus the bottom line if they were to retire in 2000, both starting at $1 million. (This chart is for illustrative purposes only and not indicative of any actual investment. The S&P 500 Index is an unmanaged index of five hundred companies used to measure large-cap US stock market performance. Investors cannot invest directly in an index.)

This graph also assumes a $36,000 ($3,000 per month) withdrawal rate increasing by 3 percent each year on both portfolios. This comparison is critical to understand because it highlights the importance of having the proper risk exposure in your late-working and early-retirement years. This stage in life is when your portfolio is the largest, and thus most vulnerable to detrimental losses. Having an all-equity portfolio would base your retirement success on luck of the draw, or what the finance industry calls "sequence of returns."

The lost decade is a devastating scenario to retire in, and we wouldn't wish that upon our worst enemy, but it's a very real scenario. As you can see, if John and Jennifer were to have retired in 2000, just ten years into retirement, their $1 million would have been cut in half, and they would be in real danger of running out of money should they not alter their lifestyle. On the flip side, if they would have retired in 2010 with that same $1 million, their portfolio would be worth over $2.5 million, a difference of over $2 million. Again, the only difference between these two retirement scenarios is the returns of the market.

Clients are shocked when they see the risk they're taking when their portfolio is predominantly composed of equities.

These situations aren't unusual. Too many people are planning in the short term, when they should be thinking about protecting their money so that it can provide for them over the next few decades.

The biggest transition you'll make is shifting your mindset from growth to a mindset of generating safe income and capital preservation. By working with us, John and Jennifer have won the game; all they need to do now is bask in the victory.

We enjoy helping couples like John and Jennifer by using a diverse mix of strategies that reduce overall portfolio risk. When your priorities shift from growth to capital preservation and income, your portfolio allocation needs to shift with it. There is no set formula on what asset mix you should have, as it will vary based on your particular needs and goals.

Our Company

This is the lifeblood of our business: shifting our clients' mindsets from accumulation mode to capital preservation and income mode, and managing their money in a way that allows them to enjoy their retirement.

Growing up in a family where your father is a financial advisor, you learn the importance of a dollar, whether you want to or not. Our father taught us at an early age the power of saving, investing, and compounding. He piqued our interest, and that interest slowly became more and more of an obsession. It eventually led to both of us committing to this field, obtaining our degrees in economics, and going on to receive the **Certified Financial Planner™** designation.

We knew about the larger investment firms out there, and the culture of those firms—the salesperson mentality. We wanted to build something different, more personal. We saw what our father was attempting to build and wanted be part of it. He specialized in retirement planning and talked to us about his vision of what he wanted this company to be. He wanted to build a company with strong values, driven by integrity, not by the almighty dollar. He did not want to be attached to a big wire house; he wanted to be a stand-alone, independent company. He wanted our loyalty to be to our clients.

So we went for it.

Shortly after we joined the industry, we started Richard W. Paul & Associates. We put our faith in God's hands and our hard work. It took many years to build what we have now, but we built our company with unquestionable integrity and honest advice. We started in one little office, with one conference room, and now have offices across the Metro Detroit area.

Not a day goes by where we don't think about where we started, and not a day goes by where we don't think about how blessed we are to work together.

Early in our careers a client told us, "Money matters, but family is priceless." We couldn't agree more. We wrote this book for all the investors who share this same outlook—the investors who have worked so hard and saved so diligently to build what they have, not only for them but for their families.

Regardless of the size of your portfolio, this book will show you how to find a financial planner you can trust and how to switch your mindset from growth to capital preservation and income. It will also help you build a goal-oriented retirement plan and help you minimize risk in your portfolio. You've been working for decades to earn your money. Now it's time to make your money work for you. This is your nest egg, and it needs to be positioned to provide for you and your family for years to come.

Three Key Takeaways

1. A new beginning. Retirement is an exciting phase of life, but uncertainty and anxiety about finances and lifestyle can come along with it.
2. Plan for retirement. Having a retirement plan is crucial for alleviating financial concerns in retirement, but planning for your lifestyle is equally important.
3. Retirement has evolved. Over the years retirement has changed, and today's retirees face tough challenges, including uncertainty about Social Security, the decline of traditional pensions, longer life expectancies, and the need for innovative financial strategies.

Questions for You

- What are your retirement goals and aspirations?
- Have you thought about how you want to spend your retirement years?
- How do you envision your financial situation in retirement?
- Do you have a clear retirement plan in place?
- How much income does your portfolio need to generate?
- Can you spend more in your golden years of retirement (the first ten years) and still be confident you won't run out of money on the back end?

Notes:

(TWO)
Ten Simple Steps
to Retirement

*Great things are not done by impulse, but by a series of
small things brought together.*

– Vincent Van Gogh

Let's take a step back for a moment and talk about the best
ways to navigate to a successful retirement. After all, the
most important aspect of retiring is getting to retirement.
People usually start thinking about retirement far too late
or focus too much on growth without thinking about all
the other things they can do to secure a happy retirement.
Before we talk about how to make that shift from planning
for retirement to retirement itself, it's critical to form a
number of best practices for your working years.

In this chapter, we've compiled our top ten tips for
getting you to retirement:

1. Set Goals and Get on the Same Page
We hosted a radio show on WJR (Midwesterners may be
familiar with this station), where we talked about everything retirement. A topic we touched on a lot is what we

call the "**retirement red zone.**" This is the ten-year period before you hit retirement, and this is the time where some important conversations need to happen about your goals and aspirations for your ideal retirement.

It's important to share your retirement goals and aspirations with your spouse to make sure you're on the same page. An easy way to start this conversation is to revisit the twelve retirement personalities in chapter 1 and discuss which categories each of you fall into. Certain categories complement each other nicely, like the "big spender" and "travel the world" categories. There's a good chance you'll find common ground in your lifestyle and retirement goals.

On the other hand, there's a chance your retirement lifestyles won't entirely match. You may find that one spouse is a "one more year" type, while the other wants to "retire yesterday." Realizing this and understanding you will need to make compromises are important steps to getting on the same page.

It's also critical to get on the same page as to the timing of retirement. Open communication is essential, and you may find that you learn a thing or two about each other. Understanding each other's ideal retirement lifestyle and recognizing the other's goals will help toward this open communication.

For example, a "quiet life" retiree may want to retire earlier; they don't have lavish spending goals, and they look forward to the stress-free life of exiting the workforce. Once you understand what you want out of retirement, and what your spouse wants out of retirement, planning for retirement becomes a whole lot easier. If you don't understand what each other wants, you may find that one spouse resents the other for retiring too early or working too long. It's critical that you sit down with your spouse and map out your short- and long-term goals. Once you've done this, and you're both on the same page, you can start building a plan that will allow you to live the retirement you've both worked so hard to achieve.

2. Take Control of Your Health and Start Planning

You might think your health doesn't fit into the discussion of planning for retirement, but being proactive when it comes to health—whether getting your annual physical or getting your daily exercise—will pay dividends in the future. You likely contribute to your retirement systematically, without even thinking about it. Your health should be the same way. A retiree today is expected to spend $275,000 over their retirement on health care. By investing in your health now and throughout retirement, you can reduce your potential for future health care costs.

Retirement Trivia

Eighty percent of retirees in better health report having a positive experience in retirement, compared to only ___ percent of those who are in poorer health.

a. 33 percent

b. 48 percent

c. 59 percent

d. 67 percent

The answer can be found on page 176.

While there are all sorts of different ways to go about saving for your health costs, contributing to a **health savings account (HSA)** is almost always a good idea if you're eligible. An HSA is triple tax advantaged: tax-deductible when you contribute, tax-deferred while it grows, and tax-free when taken out for qualified medical expenses. Odds are, you'll have medical expenses at some point in your life, so take advantage of this account while you can. Even if your employer doesn't offer an HSA, you can open an HSA at different companies, such as Fidelity, Health Equity, or Health Savings.

3. Get Out of Debt

For those carrying debt, we all know that getting out of debt is easier said than done. The average American under the age of thirty-five has between $23,000 and $30,000 of debt in the form of credit cards, student loans, auto loans, and other forms of personal debt. The average US household owes about $7,000 on credit cards. With an average 27.91 percent **annual percentage rate (APR)** on credit cards, American families are making over $1,000 in interest payments each year.[2]

If you're living with high interest debt, paying it off is one of the smartest financial moves you can make. The reason for this is simple: You're likely paying more in terms of interest than you're likely to earn by investing.

For most people it makes sense to pay off that expensive debt instead of investing at lower rates of return. Every dollar you contribute toward your debt reduces the amount of interest expense you must pay each year and every year after that. Student loan interest rates are usually lower than most other forms of unsecured debt, making the decision about whether to pay down debt instead of investing more complex.

If you're not sure whether to pay down your debt or start investing, a financial advisor can explain the advantages and disadvantages of each option and help you make the right decision for your needs.

---

2 Michelle Black, "What Is The Average Credit Card Interest Rate This Week?" *Forbes*, https://www.forbes.com/advisor/credit-cards/average-credit-card-in-terest-rate/,

4. Live Within Your Means

Living within your means seems obvious, but most Americans aren't doing it. That's why so many of us are carrying debt. Why are Americans in so much debt? Because we like to spend! Why are Americans overspending? A 2013 Gallup Poll showed that just under one in three Americans uses a household budget, let alone follows it.[3] That's a recipe for disaster.

If you don't already have a budget, it's time to make one and stick to it. If you do have a budget but aren't meeting it, it's time to reconfigure your budget or tighten your spending. It's also possible that you're spending a lot of money on things you don't use or even want. Going through your expenses, line by line, and formulating a budget you can meet is critical to spending wisely and, hopefully, investing as much as you possibly can to your retirement, your health, and your savings.

5. Automate and Index

The easiest way to invest is to automatically direct a portion of each paycheck into your investment accounts. You'll quickly get used to having less money to spend each month, and your savings will grow over time. If your employer offers a match into your retirement account, be sure to take advantage of that. That's free money!

---

3   Dennis Jacobe, "One in Three Americans Prepare a Detailed Household Budget," Gallup, June 3, 2013, https://news.gallup.com/poll/162872/ one-three-americans-prepare-detailed-household-budget.aspx.

Active management of a stock portfolio requires skill, education, and experience. Younger investors have none of these skills, and those who try will be doing nothing more than speculating. Avoid the temptations of trying out options if you can't explain what time decay is. When you're in saving and accumulation mode, it's best to **dollar cost average** into low-cost index funds or high-quality stocks that you can **buy and hold** for a long time. Index funds will allow you to diversify throughout different asset classes and sectors, without having to manage and purchase individual stocks.

6. Don't Buy Too Much of Your Company's Stock

No matter how much you love your company, avoid the temptation to invest a significant percentage of your portfolio in your employer's stock. It's better to diversify than to be loyal. If you must own some company stock, limit your exposure to no more than 3–5 percent of your portfolio. Being an employee does not give you an edge, and it never will, unless your title begins with a C (CEO, CFO, COO, etc.).

That said, if you already own company stock, don't run out and sell it. There are special tax advantages for highly appreciated stock under the **net unrealized appreciation** provision that must be evaluated by a qualified professional before taking such action.

7. Tax Diversification

Just like you diversify your portfolio between different asset classes, it's also important to consider tax diversifying your various accounts. This way, when you get to retirement, you're not stuck with everything locked into a pretax retirement account, so any expense or distribution you take is taxable.

Proposed by Senator William Roth in 1997, the **Roth individual retirement account** (Roth IRA) is still a relatively new concept. The Roth IRA allows you to contribute money into an account that grows, tax-deferred for your retirement, and allows you to take money out at retirement without paying any taxes, provided certain requirements are met. A few years later, in 2001, the Roth became a feature in 401(k)s, allowing after-tax money to be placed into these retirement accounts.

After the reduction in taxes by the Tax Cuts and Jobs Act, signed into legislation in December 2017, we can all agree that taxes are likely to increase in the future. The Roth is more advantageous the younger you are and the less income you're making. Later in your career a Roth IRA may not be an option if your income exceeds the legal limit for these highly advantageous retirement accounts. Paying the tax now while your tax bracket is lower and before the politicians raise them will ensure that you get to keep more of your hard-earned investment.

One reason people don't like contributing to retirement accounts is the penalty for early withdrawals. The nice thing about the Roth IRA is that you can always take out your contributions without any penalties.

8. Buy into Panic, Not the Opposite

We all like buying things on sale. If the stock market sells off by 5–10 percent over any given month, take your excess cash and "buy the dip." Only use excess cash, not any cash that is needed to pay bills. Make this a rule and make it systematic. No matter what, keep to this strategy. If you don't have any excess cash, wait for the next dip when you *do* have some cash to invest. Whether it's Ebola, Brexit, the meltdown in Greece, or the COVID-19 pandemic: When the market dips, try to throw some money in.

9. Evaluate Your Insurance Needs

Life and disability insurance always get overlooked. Most people don't even know what kind of coverage they have when we ask. If this sounds like you, and you have a family you're providing for, make sure you evaluate your current situation and needs immediately.

Disability Insurance

When it comes to disability insurance, you should have a policy if others depend on the income you bring in. If you're providing for your family, we highly recommend you look into your options when it comes to disability insurance.

We recommend that your disability benefit be 60–70 percent of your gross income. For that level of coverage, you can expect to pay around 3 percent of your annual salary in premiums, though the actual amount will vary based on how much coverage you buy. The benefit of your disability insurance policy should be high enough to cover your expenditures so you can cover them while you recover. Calculate your monthly expenses and go from there.

After you've considered your income and calculated your expenses, evaluate the two basic types of disability insurance: short term and long term. Both provide a benefit that replaces a portion of your income, which again, we recommend 60–70 percent. Keep in mind, these policies are bought differently and work differently, in large part because short-term needs differ from long-term needs.

Most disability is temporary, keeping a person out of the workplace for under a year. Short-term disability is designed to replace income for these shorter periods of recovery from injury or illness. Short-term disability can sometimes be obtained as part of a group insurance plan through the workplace, either as a mandatory (employer-paid) or voluntary (employee-paid) benefit. These plans usually pay a benefit for three to six months and often include rehabilitation features to help employees get back to work sooner.

Long-term disability is for injuries or illnesses that are more severe, longer lasting, or possibly permanent. Long-term disability insurance is for these situations, with a benefit designed to last for years, possibly even through retirement. While long-term disability can be available through an employer, it's also commonly purchased as an individual policy, especially by business owners, physicians, and higher-income professionals. People in these professions are often concerned about what might happen to their family's lifestyle if they were no longer able to practice their profession.

Life Insurance

Just like with disability insurance, you'll want to perform a needs analysis when evaluating life insurance. A good needs analysis takes into account your current and future expenses.

After you've totaled your current expenses, decide how long your family would need support, and multiply your annual income by that figure. The multiplier in this case might be the total number of years it would take before your youngest child completes high school. Once you know the total number of years you're planning for, you can calculate the life insurance need and build it into your plan. We recommend erring on the side of caution and over insuring to make sure your family is provided for should any unexpected costs arise.

Once you've calculated your insurance needs, we highly recommend you sit down with a qualified professional, have them lay out the different types of insurance, and go over the pros and cons of the different policies. The insurance world can be extremely complex, with no one-size-fits-all plan.

Life insurance is an integral part of any financial plan. For most of us, the well-being of our family is the number one priority in life and death. Life insurance is a tool you can use to provide for your loved ones when you're gone and is a priority for any family.

Last, but certainly not least, is personal liability insurance. This is often referred to as **umbrella liability coverage**. This insurance is relatively cheap when compared to the coverage it provides and is added through your homeowner's insurance. The purpose of an umbrella policy is to provide additional insurance coverage for claims in excess of your homeowners and auto policies.

10. Build, Monitor, and Protect Your Credit

Your credit score is an indicator of your financial health. The list of people who have an interest in your credit score seems to grow every year. Damaged credit can be costly over time.

Here are some simple steps that you can take to protect your credit:

- Check your credit report every year for free at AnnualCreditReport.com and dispute any errors. Sites like CreditKarma.com allow you to check more frequently.
- Set up payment reminders or enroll in autopay where possible to pay your bills on time.
- Avoid late charges (anything that goes to collections gets reported to the credit bureaus).

- Pay down any balances on cards (high balances relative to your total available credit ding your credit score).
- Pay off your credit cards in full each month.

As we conclude the top ten list, it's important to remember that saving and investing for retirement is important, but you also must remember that your time on this planet is unknown and limited. It breaks our hearts to see a client work all their life to finally settle into retirement and then have a health issue that hinders their retirement, or even worse, lose a spouse.

Remember to enjoy some of your hard-earned money today and know that it's okay to buy some irrational things along the way. Maybe it's something extravagant like a once-in-a-lifetime vacation or something as simple as springing for guacamole at Chipotle. Don't go too crazy, but if all you're doing is *planning* for life after work, you might be overdoing it.

Planning is critical, but you need to live in the moment as well. Take a moment to think about the things you want out of life. Do you want to give to charity? Do you want to volunteer? Do you want to buy a dream home in Florida? Do you want to take a family vacation every few years? Do you want to help save for higher education for your children or grandchildren? Whatever your personal goals are, chances are that they will take some preparation to get there.

Most of the families we work with came to us before they retired. They heard us on the radio talking about the crucial planning period and came to see us so we could assist them in building a plan to get them to and through retirement. Don't make the mistake of waiting until the last minute to think about this. Lay out your goals, formulate a plan, and let these ten simple steps help guide you to retirement.

Three Key Takeaways

1. Set goals. Setting clear retirement goals and ensuring you and your spouse are on the same page regarding your ideal retirement lifestyle is essential.

2. Think about your health. Proactive health management, including regular checkups and exercise, is vital to reduce future health care costs in retirement.

3. Get out of debt. Paying off high-interest debt should take precedence over investing, as it often yields more significant financial benefits. Consider consulting a financial advisor for guidance on managing debt and investments.

Questions for You

- Have you communicated your retirement goals and aspirations with your spouse?
- Are you on the same page as your spouse regarding your ideal retirement lifestyle?
- How can you ensure open communication and alignment with your spouse in your retirement planning?
- Are you actively managing your health and taking measures to reduce potential future health care costs in retirement?
- What steps can you take to prioritize your health and well-being as part of your retirement planning?
- What are the advantages and disadvantages of tax diversification, especially in light of potential future tax changes?

Notes:

(THREE)
Finding Happiness in Retirement

The meaning of life is to give life meaning.

– Viktor E. Frankl

Take a moment to close your eyes and picture your ideal retirement. Now, list five words that best describe what you envisioned:

1. _____

2. _____

3. _____

4. _____

5. _____

Some of the most common words we hear from our clients include:

- Fulfilled
- Love
- Freedom
- Family
- Healthy
- Long
- Relaxing
- Peaceful
- Fun
- Success
- Travel

In a 2019 study done by MIT AgeLab, 990 adults ages eighteen through ninety-one across the United States were asked to come up with five words describing "life after career." The following chart summarizes their responses.[4]

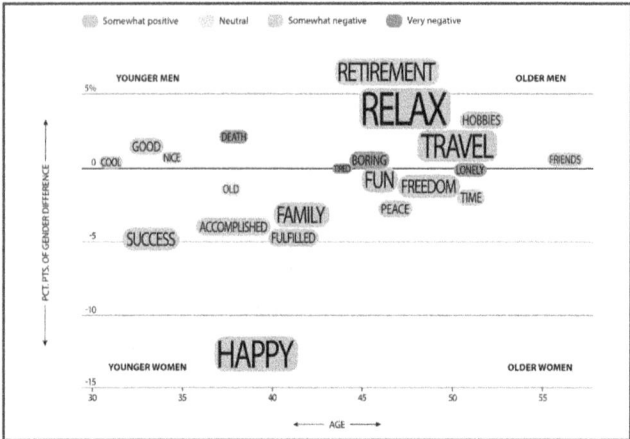

The results weren't far off from what our clients have said, and you might even find some of your answers on the chart. Surprisingly, just forty-seven words accounted for 60 percent of the responses, which are the words shown on the chart.

On the graph, age is illustrated on the x-axis, with older respondents being on the right. An interesting observation is that the word "Money" was one of younger responses (on the left), indicating that the older you are, the more likely you are to realize that money can't buy happiness. The oldest

4   Joseph F. Coughlin and Chaiwoo Lee, "The Revealing Words People Use to Describe Retirement," *The Wall Street Journal*, November 17, 2019, https://www.wsj.com/articles/the-revealing-words-people-use-to-describe-retirement-11574046240.

answer was "Friends," which could tell us that the older you get, the more value you put on relationships.

The y-axis illustrates the difference in words by gender. You can see the most male-dominated answer at the top, "Retirement." This either illustrates that men are extremely simple, or terrible at following instructions, or likely some combination of the two. On the contrary, the most female-dominated answer, by an overwhelming margin, was "Happy."

Sorry, guys, but we agree with the women on this one. A happy retirement is what you worked all your life for. A happy retirement is what will give you a sense of fulfillment when all is said and done. But in order be happy in retirement, you first need to understand the science of what makes you happy.

What Is Happiness?

On the surface, happiness is a simple concept. The definition of happiness is the state of being happy. But we can all agree that achieving true happiness isn't that simple. Philosophers and psychologists have been debating the science of happiness for thousands of years. There are two basic philosophies: hedonic and eudaimonic, both originating from ancient Greek philosophy.

To explain these two philosophies, we'll defer to an excerpt from a ThoughtCo.com article by psychology expert Cynthia Vinney, PhD.

Origins of the Concept of Hedonic Happiness

The idea of hedonic happiness dates back to the fourth century B.C., when a Greek philosopher, Aristippus, taught that the ultimate goal in life should be to maximize pleasure. Throughout history, a number of philosophers have adhered to this hedonic viewpoint, including Hobbes and Bentham. Psychologists who study happiness from a hedonic perspective cast a wide net by conceptualizing hedonia in terms of pleasures of both the mind and body. In this view, then, happiness involves maximizing pleasure and minimizing pain.

In American culture, hedonic happiness is often championed as the ultimate goal. Popular culture tends to portray an outgoing, social, joyous view of life, and as a result, Americans often believe that hedonism in its various forms is the best way to achieve happiness.

Origins of the Concept of Eudaimonic Happiness

Eudaimonic happiness gets less attention in American culture as a whole but is no less important in the psychological research of happiness and well-being. Like hedonia, the concept of eudaimonia dates back to the fourth century B.C., when Aristotle first proposed it in his work, *Nicomachean Ethics*. According to Aristotle, to achieve happiness, one should live their life in accordance with their virtues. He claimed that people are constantly striving to meet their potential and be their best selves, which leads to greater purpose and meaning.

Like the hedonic perspective, a number of philosophers aligned themselves with the eudaimonic perspective, including Plato, Marcus Aurelius, and Kant. Psychological theories like Maslow's hierarchy of needs, which points to self-actualization as the highest goal in life, champion a eudaimonic perspective on human happiness and flourishing.[5]

Most experts would agree that some combination of the above two philosophies is the optimal way to live a happy life. The hedonic approach allows you to feel a sense of accomplishment when you buy something nice, achieve a goal, or experience a major life event. The eudaimonic promotes living a holistic life with strong morals and helping others along the way.

We've taken the time to explain the science behind happiness because we often see retirees make the mistake of running on the hedonic treadmill for their retirement. The hedonic treadmill is a theory in which experiences, positive or negative, result in a corresponding change of emotion, in which the emotion eventually wears off, and you return to your normal resting state of happiness. The key here is that

---

5   Cynthia Vinney, "What's the Difference Between Eudaimonic and Hedonic Happiness?" ThoughtCo.com, updated February 13, 2020, https://www. thoughtco.com/eudaimonic-and-hedonic-happiness-4783750.

hedonic happiness typically results in a temporary state of happiness.

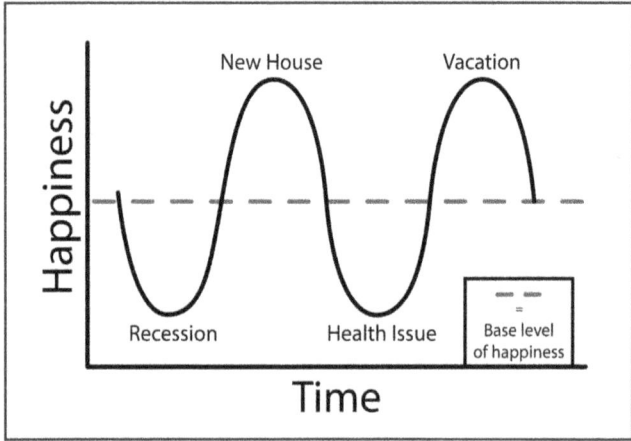

Like Dr. Vinney explained, American culture tends to focus on hedonic happiness, whether that be a new phone or a new car or money in general. Living a lifestyle focused on hedonic happiness won't make you feel fulfilled long term.

Think about your working years. A common goal might to be focus on your portfolio size. Your goal might be to save $100,000 or $1 million, and it sure feels great to see your portfolio size add another digit or a comma. But once you hit that goal, you can't sustain that feeling, and you'll find yourself chasing a larger number. And the problem with numbers is that they can always be higher.

A study in 1978 in *The Journal of Personality and Social Psychology* showed that lottery winners were much happier immediately after winning the lottery, but within months they returned to their pre-lottery state of happiness.[6] Maybe the old saying is right: Money can't buy happiness.

So to balance hedonic happiness, one should live a more eudaimonic life, including building better relationships with family and friends, engaging in your passions, living a healthy lifestyle, mentoring, volunteering, practicing gratitude, meditating, and learning new skills. Hedonic experiences are, without a doubt, a critical component to happiness but only provide a temporary feeling of satisfaction. When these experiences are paired with a eudaimonic lifestyle, you can best optimize your happiness in retirement.

Recognizing that the ultimate goal of retirement is happiness, you can now understand that your primary goal is no longer maximum growth on your money. Too many retirees stay stuck in the growth world, maintaining a portfolio with a high percentage of equities. In a way, we feel it's the advisor's job to assist the clients in establishing clear goals for retirement. Once these goals are established, we can then go to work developing a plan that will meet these goals. But sometimes, the advisor is only focused on growing the money, when they should be more focused on the true goals of the client, which typically in retirement is generating income or preserving capital.

And here lies the problem: In the world of financial planning, there are primarily two types of advisors: growth

---

6   Philip Brickman, Dan Coates, and Ronnie Janoff-Bulman, (1978) "Lottery winners and accident victims: Is happiness relative?" *Journal of Personality and Social Psychology*, 36(8), 917–927, https://doi.org/10.1037/0022-3514.36.8.917.

advisors and retirement advisors. Just as financial strategies have evolved over time, such as the Roth IRA or income annuities, the financial industry has evolved, with retirement planning emerging as its own distinctive field within the industry.

Most people who come to us are working with growth advisors who are investing to reach for the highest possible returns on their money. In your working years, this makes sense. A growth advisor's job is to get the best return on your investment portfolio; you're not focused on generating income and have a longer time horizon. You only have so many working years to invest in your retirement, so you want to maximize the growth on the money you invest.

There's a common expression that epitomizes your run-of-the-mill growth advisor: "If the only tool you have is a hammer, then everything starts to look like a nail." Growth advisors might only be licensed to use market-based strategies to grow your money, which is great when you're in growth mode, but not necessarily the best fit for your retirement nest egg. If they're only licensed for securities, they might not be able to recommend the strategy that best fits your needs. Advisors can be biased in their recommendations if they have limited tools in their toolbox, and in chapter 9 we'll discuss financial advisor biases.

When you enter the retirement red zone, your goals begin to shift and become twofold. One, you want to protect your money so that you know you're secure in your retirement. Two, you want to develop a plan that focuses on producing income from your portfolio to supplement your guaranteed income streams (Social Security and pension).

Changing Your Mindset

Our job as retirement planners is to change our clients' mindsets from growth to capital preservation and income.

This transition can be difficult for some at first. They've been told their entire working lives that their portfolio needs to get the best returns possible, and now we're telling them to look for a more conservative return of roughly 4–7 percent. Why?

Simple. We live in uncertain times. We *always* live in uncertain times. Ten years in the future will be as uncertain as tomorrow, and we could see more financial crises, like those that hit in the early 2000s or in 2008, or another pandemic that shuts down life as we know it. A lot of retirees think their retirement will only last fifteen to twenty years, when it could last thirty or more. That's more than enough time for another major event to derail your retirement if you're taking too much risk.

The first question you should be asking about your allocation is "How much can this portfolio lose in a bad year?"—not "How much can this portfolio make on a good year?"

The last thing you want to do is risk losing what you've been working for years to build. Having an all-equity portfolio during your retirement is even more dangerous because you likely have more money to lose now than at any other time in your life.

Think of retirement as a mountain. All your working years you've been climbing and climbing. Sure, you've stumbled along the way, but you finally reach the summit. Now that you're at the top of the mountain, you must safely descend. If you make a mistake, you have a long way to fall—farther than ever before. The climb down is more dangerous than the climb up; once you start falling, gravity pulls you down, faster and faster.

Your portfolio works the same way. A loss while taking income is a major problem. Before, while you were working, a market correction meant you had the ability to buy shares at a discount. Now, a market correction means you may be forced to sell at a low. Your portfolio already has the momentum of withdrawals being taken from it, so adding in a market correction can be devastating to the long-term sustainability of your portfolio.

A **market-based portfolio** can do just fine if you catch the right time period, but this isn't the time to take that risk. Remember, your portfolio has the greatest risk of loss at the end of your working years and beginning of your retirement years. For most investors, this is when your portfolio peaks in value, and this is the point in your life where you should be making the transition from growth to income.

In chapter 1, we discussed sequence of returns risk with the case study of John and Jennifer. If you see high returns in your early years of retirement, then you're in a great position. If you see negative returns in your early years, you're in trouble. We refer to this as the luck of the draw. Most people don't want their retirement plans based on luck; they want them based on math.

At this stage of the game, there's no need to take unnecessary risks with your money. There are conservative strategies that are much safer and more focused on generating the income you'll need to enjoy your retirement.

Good retirement planners will educate clients on the types of conservative investments available, and they'll show them how shifting their riskier investments into a more conservative strategy will benefit them. Plenty of strategies have a history of consistent, risk-averse returns. Unfortunately, many financial advisors continue taking unnecessary risks for their clients in retirement. People who come to us for advice often believe their portfolio is conservative when they're actually taking more risk than they think.

When we say that you need to make a shift from growth to income, that doesn't mean your entire portfolio. At our firm we help our clients identify the amount of their portfolio that they'll need to shift to income-focused so they can generate what is needed to meet their retirement goals. Once we're safely and efficiently generating the income they need to meet their expenses, we can bring on more risk and go after additional growth with the remainder of their portfolio.

Retirement Trivia

If your portfolio loses 40 percent of its value, you'll need to make a gain of more than ____ percent to get back to even.

a. 40 percent
b. 50 percent
c. 66.67 percent
d. 100 percent

The answer can be found on page 177.

Case Study

Nancy is a sixty-seven-year-old widow with a $900,000 portfolio and a Social Security benefit of $2,500 a month. With four kids and several grandchildren, her primary goal was to spend more time with her family and leave a healthy inheritance to her children. Her health wasn't great, so she wanted to make the most of her retirement years without squandering her retirement assets.

Nancy, like most new clients who walk through our doors, was focused on protecting and preserving her assets rather than maximizing growth and taking on unnecessary risk. "I want to make sure I don't lose what I worked so hard for," she said. "I want enough money to see my family, and I'd like to leave some money to them." Like a lot of people starting families and working their way into their careers, her kids were struggling financially. It was important to Nancy that her children be taken care of.

The first thing we did with Nancy, like we do with all new clients, was run a "stress test" on her portfolio. We always want to see what sort of allocation new clients are invested in and determine how much risk they're actually taking. Nancy had informed us that she wanted a downside of no more than 10 percent, and she didn't care about missing out on market returns. She was now in retirement and was more so focused on not losing money.

Sure enough, though Nancy's advisor had informed her that her portfolio was moderately conservative, she was taking far more risk than she was comfortable with. Her portfolio was primarily invested in equities and various other investments that have been hit hard in the past. These would have been good investments if Nancy's goal was to take risk and grow her portfolio as much as possible. But Nancy's goals were to grow her funds conservatively while preserving capital. She wanted to live comfortably in her retirement and leave her family with a healthy inheritance.

When we showed Nancy that she could lose nearly half her portfolio if another recession were to strike, she was shocked. That was exactly what Nancy *didn't* want. Nancy's approach, of course, doesn't work for all our clients. Many are comfortable taking on greater risk for greater return. This was not the case for Nancy. She had no tolerance for risk; she was only interested in preservation. Yet, there she was, taking unnecessary risk.

It's important to understand in a case like this, the **risk capacity** of the client versus the **risk tolerance**. Risk capacity and risk tolerance are two key concepts in financial planning that help individuals assess and manage their investment risk effectively. Risk capacity refers to the ability of an individual to withstand potential financial losses without experiencing significant adverse effects on their financial plan. It is influenced by factors such as income, assets, liabilities, time horizon, and overall financial stability. In contrast, risk tolerance refers to an individual's psychological willingness or comfort level with taking on investment risk. It reflects an individual's attitudes, preferences, and emotions towards risk and can vary significantly from person to person. While risk capacity focuses on objective financial factors, such as financial resources and goals, risk tolerance is more subjective and influenced by personal factors, such as temperament, past experiences, and future expectations. In Nancy's case, she had the capacity to take on risk, but not the tolerance to withstand the whims of the market.

What we did with Nancy was take a **bucketing** approach, like we do with all our clients. We established a more conservative bucket of money that would generate an extra $1,500 of monthly income. We established another bucket to provide additional income later in life, if needed, for future health care or long-term care costs. The last bucket was for her children. She was perfectly fine investing this for growth, like the previous advisor had her positioned, because this money had a purpose. The purpose was to grow this as much as possible to transfer to her kids.

Nancy's risk exposure is now in line with her risk tolerance. She has the steady income she needs to enjoy her retirement and leave a healthy inheritance to her children. More importantly, she has peace of mind knowing she has a plan in place.

When we put Nancy's case under the microscope, we discovered that her advisor had several pending lawsuits and had settled multiple times for questionable practices.

We see that a lot. Financial planning is a complicated business, yet almost anyone can call themselves a financial planner. This is why it's important you do your homework when selecting an advisor. Otherwise, you could be working with someone who is licensed in only one area of financial planning and doesn't have the knowledge to guide you through retirement. Two great resources are BrokerCheck by FINRA (Financial Industry Regulatory Authority) or the Security and Exchange Committee's investment advisor search, which provides a background on the advisor's history, including any investment complaints.

Intelligent, trustworthy retirement planners do exist. So why not do a little research and shop around before choosing your retirement planner? Like receiving a diagnosis from a doctor, it's always wise to seek a second opinion. We were happy to be Nancy's second opinion.

Everyone has a different story and different desires for their nonworking years. It's a delight to get to know our clients and their goals for retirement. We enjoy educating them in the various ways they can accomplish their goals, and more.

A small mistake can cost you thousands upon thousands of dollars. When you're dealing with your life savings, each move must be calculated and concise. It all adds up, whether it's selling a stock with a gain, naming your beneficiaries, or filing for Social Security. A miscalculated financial move at this stage of your life can be devastating.

We've seen it happen. We had a client misfile her Social Security benefits. Now that the issue is fixed after analyzing and refiling her benefits, she receives an extra $600 a month from Social Security, in addition to the $27,000 in back pay she received when her filing was corrected. Over a span of thirty years, that's over $250,000. When we asked her what she was going to spend all that extra money on, she said, "My grandchildren!"

The financial world is extraordinarily complicated. It's easy to miss things like a mistake in your Social Security benefit and lose out.

As advisors, we like to know that our clients' essential expenses will be covered in retirement. We protect the core of our clients' portfolios so that they can generate the income they need for their retirement expenses, such as traveling, spending time with family, helping their kids with finances, and taking care of themselves when health events occur.

After we've protected the core of a client's retirement, we focus the rest of their portfolio on growth so that they can leave their family in the best possible position. Some of our clients, however, have extremely healthy portfolios and can take on more risk.

We do invest portfolios with the primary goal of long-term growth, but only under the right circumstances, and only with a proper time horizon. The market is volatile even when it's doing well. No financial advisor can predict the future. We never know when or what will trigger a downturn in the market that could destroy your retirement plan if you're taking on too much risk and not protecting enough of your capital. While retirement planners have no way of foreseeing the short-term behavior of the market, a good retirement planner will make sure your income is protected in the short term before going after long-term growth.

Remember, just as a seasoned mountain climber carefully navigates the descent, balancing each step to avoid the pitfalls below, so too should you secure your financial foothold as you approach your retirement journey.

Three Key Takeaways

1. Happiness is the ultimate goal. The common words and sentiments associated with retirement include "fulfilled," "family," "relaxing," "success," and "love." A happy retirement is seen as the key to fulfillment, but it requires understanding the science of what makes one happy.

2. Balance hedonic and eudaimonic happiness. Two philosophies of happiness have to be balanced: hedonic and eudaimonic. Hedonic happiness focuses on maximizing pleasure and minimizing pain, often through material and external experiences. Eudaimonic happiness focuses on living in accordance with virtues and achieving one's potential for a greater purpose. A combination of both philosophies is optimal for a happy retirement.

3. Shift from growth to capital preservation and income. Retirees often need to transition from a growth-focused investment strategy to one that emphasizes capital preservation and income generation. Once you reach retirement, your primary goal shifts from maximizing returns to protecting your savings and producing income.

Questions for You

- What are the key components of your ideal retirement, and do they align with the common sentiments expressed by others who have considered their retirement goals and aspirations?
- Which philosophy of happiness—hedonic or eudaimonic—resonates more with your retirement aspirations, and how can you incorporate elements of both into your retirement planning for long-term happiness?
- Have you evaluated your investment portfolio to ensure it aligns with your retirement goals, particularly the need for capital preservation and income generation?
- Are you prepared for potential market downturns that could impact your retirement income and lifestyle?

Notes:

FOUR

Risks to a Successful Retirement

*Hope for the best, prepare for the worst,
and expect the unexpected.*

– Zig Ziglar

Retirees encounter five primary risks, many of which they're unaware of or do not anticipate. A successful retirement plan addresses these risks and attempts to mitigate them. The first risk, market risk, was discussed in the previous chapters. You need to make sure your portfolio isn't overly allocated to equities, a certain asset class, or a certain sector because your retirement plan will be at the mercy of the markets. Other risks you need to understand when planning for retirement are longevity, inflation, poor tax planning, and health care.

Longevity Risk

Arguably the most difficult risk to plan for, longevity risk refers to the unpredictability of how long an individual or couple will live. While increasing life expectancy is a positive development, it also introduces financial planning challenges. Retirees who live too long face the risk of outliving their assets and may need to support themselves for longer than they anticipated. This risk can result in the depletion of funds that lead to financial difficulties and potentially relying on limited Social Security benefits. To mitigate this risk, retirees must carefully strategize their investments and factor in potential health care costs associated with aging.

A 2014 article in the *Journal of Financial Planning* describes a "retirement consumption puzzle." It explains how retirees tend to spend more in their early years of retirement because they're enjoying their prime, nonworking years. Their spending tends to dip in the middle years of retirement as discretionary expenses like travel decrease. In their later years, expenses again increase because of health care and other costs of aging. This is referred to as the *retirement spending smile.*[7]

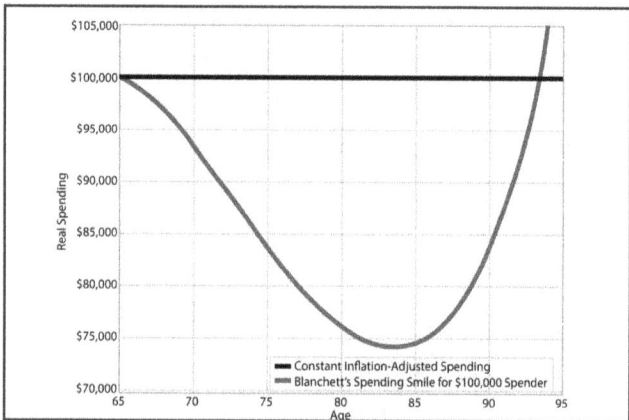

7   David Blanchett, CFP, "Exploring the Retirement Consumption Puzzle," Financial Planning Association, *Journal of Financial Planning*, May 2014, https://www.financialplanningassociation.org/article/journal/MAY14-exploring-retirement-consumption-puzzle.

As you can see, there are three distinct phases of retirement. In the book *The Prosperous Retirement*, Michael Stein refers to these three phases as the Go-Go Years, the Slow-Go Years, and the No-Go Years.[8] The first phase of retirement is the most active you'll ever be and where you have the most energy to travel and enjoy your free time. In the second phase, you start to slow down and spend less on discretionary expenses. In the last phase, expenses begin to increase again to cover the additional health care costs that naturally come with getting older. In our experience working with retirees, we tend to agree with Michael Stein's assessment.

The most common way to combat longevity risk is with guaranteed lifetime income streams, such as pensions and Social Security. A pension is a stream of income payments that are paid out to you as long as you're living. Pensions are not a new concept. They've been around since ancient Rome, where soldiers were guaranteed paychecks after they were finished serving. Of course, the typical life expectancy at that time wasn't much more than forty, so it wasn't too much of a commitment back then.

Pensions in the United States began at the country's founding, with various payment commitments being made to veterans of the Revolutionary War. A century later American Express became the first private sector company to offer a pension in 1875. Fast forward another century

---

8 Michael Stein, *The Prosperous Retirement: Guide to the New Reality* (Emstco Press, 1998).

and more than 50 percent of private sector workers had a pension.

After pensions began failing, the government decided to step in and enact the **Employee Retirement Income Security Act,** which created the defined benefit and defined contribution plans we know today. Over the last few decades, companies have shifted to a defined contribution structure, such as a **401(k),** leading to a reduction in pension commitments and, more notably, shifting the burden of generating retirement income to the retiree. In recent years companies have even started buying retirees out of their pensions by offering a present-day lump sum of money to take them off the hook for a lifetime of payments.

If you receive the option to take your pension as a lump sum, you must consult a qualified advisor. This is likely the single biggest financial decision you'll ever face. A MetLife survey showed that about one-fifth of retirement-plan participants surveyed who received pensions or 401(k)s as lump sums depleted that money in an average of five years.[9]

Being in the finance industry, we believe this statistic. The retirees we sit down with often want to spend more money up-front during their golden years of retirement (ages sixty to seventy-five). This makes perfect sense since you don't know how long you're going to be in good health. But this also presents some difficult challenges on the back

---

9   "Retirees Depleting Retirement Plan Lump Sums Faster Than Five Years Ago," MetLife, February 23, 2022, https://metlife-prod-2019.adobecqms.net/about-us/newsroom/2022/february/retirees-depleting-retirement-plan-lump-sums-faster-than-five-years-ago/.

end of retirement because of longevity risk. We call this a "tiered retirement," as your expenses will be higher on the front-end, then slightly lowering as those expenses drop off, as you check those boxes off on the travel destinations, and you begin to slow down.

Then on the back end, most people don't factor in the rising costs of health care, and they don't plan for inflation. You must plan for these. Make sure you have income streams that will be there to take care of you should your life expectancy be longer than anticipated.

According to the Society of Actuaries, a couple who is aged sixty-five today has a 50 percent chance that one of them will live to age ninety-three.[10] See the image below:

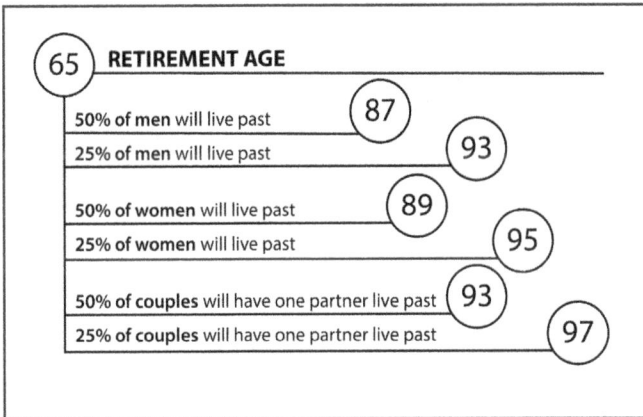

(65) **RETIREMENT AGE**

50% of men will live past (87)
25% of men will live past (93)

50% of women will live past (89)
25% of women will live past (95)

50% of couples will have one partner live past (93)
25% of couples will have one partner live past (97)

---

10   Insured Retirement Institute, "State of the Insured Retirement Industry," February 2020, 22.

Consider yourself lucky if you have a pension. Those who do not have a pension must rely on Social Security and their investments to meet their retirement income needs.

Let's discuss the history of Social Security and the different decisions that must be made.

Franklin D. Roosevelt enacted the **Social Security Act (SSA)** on the cusp of the Great Depression (1929–1935). It promised relief to millions of elderly and retired Americans. Social Security provided benefits for retirement, aid to dependent children, and insurance for the disabled or the unemployed.

Retirement Trivia

On January 31, 1940, the first monthly retirement check was issued to Ida May Fuller of Ludlow, Vermont. Ida paid a total of $24.75 into the Social Security program.

How much was paid out to her in Social Security benefits?

  a. $28

  b. $228

  c. $2,228

  d. $22,228

The answer can be found on page179.

Understanding Social Security

Today, Social Security benefits represent on average a third of retirees' income. Nearly 90 percent of Americans who are sixty-five and older receive some type of Social Security benefit. About half of married couples and 71 percent of unmarried people on Social Security rely on the benefits for at least 50 percent of their incomes. Nearly a quarter of married couples and about 43 percent of unmarried people rely on Social Security for at least 90 percent of their income.

The **Bipartisan Budget Act of 2015** closed two complex filing loopholes available to married couples. The loopholes allowed some married people to begin receiving spousal benefits at their **full retirement age (FRA),** while their own Social Security benefits continued to grow by delaying filing for it (a strategy commonly referred to as *file and suspend*).

Your benefit amount varies depending on when you apply for benefits; the earliest you can claim is at age sixty-two and the latest you can claim is age seventy. If you claim prior to reaching your full FRA, the SSA reduces your benefit amount by a percentage for each month prior to your full retirement age. For example, if you were born in 1960 and retire at age sixty-two (2023), you'll get 70 percent of your full retirement age monthly benefit. This number slowly increases every year you delay your benefit.

Full retirement age varies. The full retirement age is sixty-six years and two months for those born in 1955. The age gradually increases to sixty-seven for people born in

1960 and later. If retirees take benefits prior to their FRA, their benefits will be permanently reduced. The full retirement age is when recipients will be able to receive their full benefits (or 100 percent of their calculated benefits).

Following legislative changes in 1983, the full retirement age, which was sixty-five, began rising by two months starting for people born in 1938. But benefits will increase by 8 percent per year for those who delay collecting Social Security beyond their FRA. Recipients who wait until they're seventy to collect benefits will receive 24 percent higher payments.

Both choices (retiring early at sixty-two or delaying until seventy) have advantages and disadvantages. The SSA calculates individual benefits so that recipients receive approximately the same total amount during their retirement.

This is a decision that shouldn't be made quickly. There is no perfect way to take Social Security, and you should weigh all your options to find the best strategy for your specific needs. Sit with an advisor and discuss the tax implications, longevity concerns, future loss of a spouse and the effect that would have, and reduction of benefits if taken improperly. For those under full retirement age, the SSA sets outside earning limits for recipients who receive benefits. When you exceed those limits, the SSA reduces your Social Security benefits.

The SSA deducts one dollar in benefits for every two dollars above the outside income limit if you're working and collecting Social Security prior to your full retirement age. In the year you reach full retirement age, the SSA subtracts one dollar in benefits for every three dollars above the limit. That deduction, however, only applies in the months of that year prior to the month you reach full retirement age.

In the month you reach your full retirement age, the SSA no longer restricts your outside earnings.

Pensions and Social Security provide guaranteed income streams that last as long as you do. When we're building a plan, we plan for our clients to live to one hundred years old. Think how far medical technology has come in the last few decades. It will only continue to get better and allow for longer lives and longer retirements. But a longer life presents bigger planning challenges.

Inflation Risk

Inflation is defined as an increase in price that causes a corresponding reduction in the purchasing power of your money. In the short term it's not a big deal. Remember that five-dollar footlong from Subway? Remember how it became the seven-dollar footlong, then the nine-dollar footlong, and now the eleven-dollar footlong? Not the end of the world but nevertheless frustrating for frequent Subway goers. Not everything can be a beacon of stability like the $1.50 Costco hotdog-and-soda combo. As part of our meticulous research for this book, we went back to collect nearly forty years of data to recreate the following price chart:

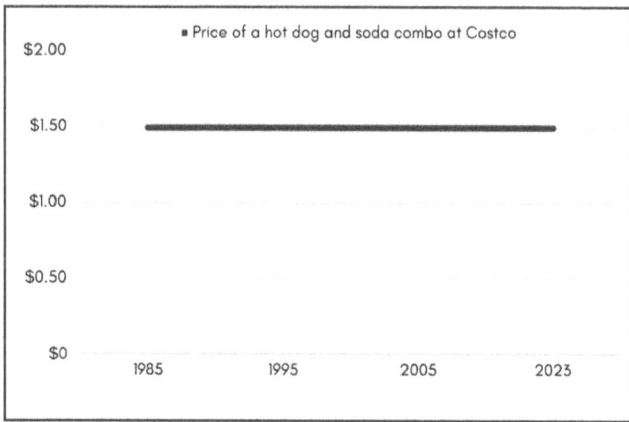

To be fair, Costco did eliminate that delightful little onion machine, and that was certainly a frustrating change. Nevertheless, in the long-term, inflation can have a huge impact. A $50,000 budget at 3 percent inflation will erode to $37,400 in purchasing power in just ten years.

The **Federal Reserve** targets a 2 percent level of inflation for the US economy, which encourages spending, avoids deflation, and supports borrowing and lending. Most importantly, 2 percent inflation isn't noticeable on a year-to-year basis for consumers. That 2 percent level seems to work well for everyone. But there will be time periods where inflation runs wild. Let's look at what happened from 2020 to 2023 as a recent example.

Everything was great in January 2020. The sun was shining, and the market was off to a great start, but then clouds started to roll in. In March we saw the quickest 30 percent downturn as a result of the mass panic of COVID-19. Nobody wanted to leave their home in fear of the virus, which led to all-time highs in unemployment. The signs were obvious—we were surely going into a recession, right?

Wrong.

We had a record recovery, and returns were off the charts, but nobody was asking how this was possible. To be blunt, we kicked the can down the road. The government injected trillions of dollars into the economy to keep us out of a recession, and it worked. Everything was good; actually everything was great. You couldn't go wrong picking any stock or high-growth investment. We were all a bunch of pale, stock-picking gurus who never left our homes unless we were stepping out on our porch to grab a silly purchase we made from Amazon. What could possibly go wrong? Well . . . inflation.

We talked about how you don't feel inflation at 2 percent, but you certainly feel it at 10+ percent. We went from filling up our cars for forty dollars, to spending nearly a hundred dollars. Inflation was out of control, and something needed to be done. We again turned to our friends over at the Fed, but this time they didn't hand us more money. We were told they needed to fix the inflation problem and began a much stricter monetary policy. Jerome Powell, the Fed chair, instantly went from superhero to villain, through quantitative tightening and raising the federal funds rate. In short, the Fed needed to inflict pain into the economy and stunt economic growth to curb inflation. The following chart shows the Consumer Price Index spike and the subsequent decline from 2021 to 2024.[11]

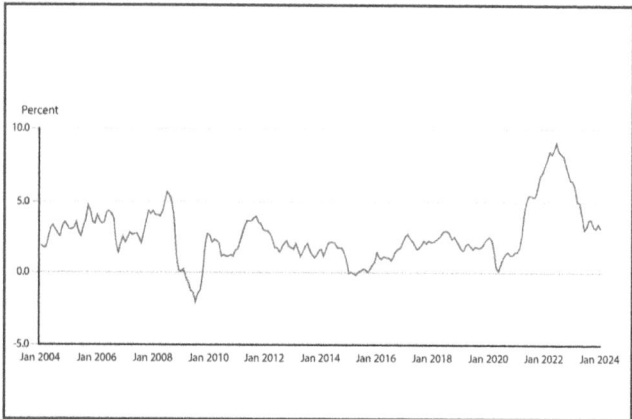

As you can see, the **Consumer Price Index (CPI)** over the last decade has averaged approximately 2.6 percent, and going back over 109 years, this number jumps to 3.3 percent.

Fortunately, retirees received a cost-of-living adjustment (COLA) of 5.9 percent in 2022, 8.7 percent in 2023, and 3.2 percent in 2024. Unfortunately, most pensions lack COLAs, drastically reducing the purchasing power of these income streams over time.

Since automatic annual COLAs began in 1975, the average cost-of-living increase has been 3.76 percent. Over the past twenty-five years, retirees have seen just over two-thirds that number, at 2.58 percent. Going forward, we

---

11 "12-Month Percentage Change, Consumer Price Index, selected categories," U.S. Bureau of Labor Statistics, https://www.bls.gov/charts/consumer-price-index/consumer-price-index-by-category-line-chart.htm.

wouldn't be surprised to see the cost-of-living adjustment average in the 2 percent range.

Year	COLA	Year	COLA
2000	2.50%	2013	1.70%
2001	3.50%	2014	1.50%
2002	2.60%	2015	1.70%
2003	1.40%	2016	0.00%
2004	2.10%	2017	0.30%
2005	2.70%	2018	2.00%
2006	4.10%	2019	2.80%
2007	3.30%	2020	1.60%
2008	2.30%	2021	1.30%
2009	5.80%	2022	5.90%
2010	0.00%	2023	8.70%
2011	0.00%	2024	3.20%
2012	3.60%	Average:	2.58%

Source: Social Security Administration, "Cost of Living Adjustments," https://www.ssa.gov/oact/cola/colaseries.html.

Inflation is a sneaky risk to your retirement because it's something you don't notice on a year-to-year basis. Given that more and more retirees are living into their nineties, twenty-five to thirty years of inflation can become a major problem at the back end of retirement and needs to be properly planned for.

The assets that are most subject to inflation risk are your cash and cash equivalents. Anything that typically returns less than 3 percent may not be keeping up with inflation. That's not to say that you shouldn't have any money in your bank, because you should. We recommend six to twelve months of expenses in an emergency account. Beyond that, you may have too much exposure to inflation risk.

A lot of times prospective clients have excess bank funds because they're scared. They're scared to put it in the market since they've lost out on recent market gains. They're scared to put it in bonds because of rising interest rates. They're scared to lock it into anything with a time commitment in case they need access to it. They're scared of trusting anyone or anything with the money they've worked so hard for.

There are safe alternatives to get your money working harder, such as short-term bonds or Treasury inflation-protected securities (TIPS). For liquidity purposes, we consider short-term bond funds a nice "back up" to your bank account. We'll set this up for our clients so they have an account readily available if their bank assets were to be depleted. These accounts aren't exciting but can generate a more stable return even in bad markets or with rising interest rates because of their short-term nature. You can also consider TIPS, which are issued by the US government and linked to the rate of inflation. They pay a nominal rate of interest and adjust their value with the declared rate of inflation. If the nominal rate of interest was 2 percent, and inflation was 3 percent, you would receive a return of 5 percent. TIPS are not a cure-all to inflation but may be a better alternative to sitting in cash or CDs, since you have a fighting chance of keeping up with inflation. Keep in mind, there are some years where the government may declare no inflation or even negative inflation (deflation).

These are a couple of ways to combat inflation with little risk. When it comes to portfolio design in retirement and building an income plan, factoring in inflation is just as important as factoring in market risk. Your advisor should be talking to you about inflation—it could be a silent retirement killer if ignored.

Although the above example may be aggressive, inflation can still be devastating if it isn't properly planned for. When we're building a plan, we take a more conservative approach by assuming continued inflation throughout retirement. It's always better to err on the side of caution for planning purposes.

Retirement Trivia

What term describes the phenomenon where manufacturers reduce the size or quantity of a product while keeping its price the same?

a. Disinflation

b. Shrinkflation

c. Deflation

d. Miniaturization

The answer can be found on page 178.

Health Care Risk

Some expenses don't inflate from year to year, like a fixed mortgage, and some expenses inflate more than the average inflation rate. Unfortunately, for retirees, health care tends to increase in costs from year to year at a higher rate than other expenses, closer to 5 percent. Future costs of a health care event are the most difficult puzzle pieces to place when building a retirement plan. Some retirees have already planned for this, either by buying a **long-term care** policy or saving as much as possible in a health savings account. Most retirees have no plan for a future health care event at all.

There are four standard ways to plan for a health care event:

Long-Term Care Insurance

Not the most exciting option, but long-term care insurance is a simple way to plan for health care costs. If you're older, have an illness, or have a family history, you may not be insurable. The ideal time to get a long-term care insurance policy is in your late fifties or early sixties. Most people don't like paying a monthly premium for something they may or may not use, especially when it costs as much as these policies. Most people who have a long-term care policy have witnessed firsthand how devastating the costs of a long-term care event can be. Certain provisions need to be discussed with a qualified financial professional to factor in things such as premium increases and cost-of-living adjustments.

Self-Insuring

The self-pay option means you can fund a potential long-term health care event out of your own pocket—either from retirement funds or a separate bucket set aside for these costs. This tends to be an appealing option for retirees because it doesn't have the use-it-or-lose-it provision mentioned above. If you don't end up needing the money for health care costs, it passes on to your beneficiaries.

The big question for the self-insuring option is how much do you need? Health care costs can vary wildly depending on your location and type of care. Here in Michigan, the median cost for a semiprivate nursing home is approximately $8,000 per month. Take an $8,000 per month cost and expand that over three years, and you're paying $288,000 for your health care needs. Although self-insuring might be the preferred option, most people can't afford to go that route.

Health Care Riders on Annuities or Life Insurance

Most people want to avoid Medicaid at all costs. The government doesn't want you to go on **Medicaid** either; it's expensive for them. **Medicare** is primarily funded through payroll taxes while Medicaid is jointly funded by the federal government and individual states. As part of the **Pension Protection Act of 2006**, Congress enacted an incentive to keep you off Medicaid and provide additional coverage for health care costs. The act also introduced *health care riders* as an additional feature to a life insurance or annuity policy.

Life insurance pays a lump sum at death, and annuities pay a stream of income while you're living. These extra features are health care riders that can be added to annuities and life insurance policies to allow you early access to the death benefit or enhance your income if a long-term care event occurs. Since there is no underwriting for annuity contracts, these health care riders can be attractive for those with existing medical issues. With life insurance, this rider is often referred to as a chronic care rider, and in annuities it is commonly referred to as a home health care rider.

Trust Planning

Trust planning isn't used often, since this strategy involves moving your assets from your estate into an irrevocable trust, which limits your access to these funds. An **irrevocable trust** protects your assets from a potential spenddown, but it also involves you going on Medicaid and into a Medicaid facility, which is likely not where your loved ones want you to spend your final years. To implement this strategy, you need to seek out an estate planner who specializes in this area.

Your retirement planner should educate you in these different ways to help you plan for a long-term care event. Then you can make an educated decision rather than take a shot in the dark.

For those who think a long-term care event is unlikely throughout your retirement, look at the stats:

- Do you have homeowners insurance in case of a fire? If so, the chances of your home burning down is 1 in 1,200, or 0.08 percent.
- Do you have auto insurance in case of an accident? If so, the chances of your car being totaled is 1 in 240, or 0.4 percent.
- Do you have a plan in place in case of a long-term care event? If not, the chances of a long-term care event are 1 in 2, or 50 percent. It makes little sense to insure your home and car but not yourself.

Tax Risk

The final risk most retirees don't consider is tax risk (i.e., poor tax planning). As we know, pensions are less common today than they used to be, as companies have shifted the burden of saving for retirement onto retirees through the use of 401(k)s and other similarly defined contribution plans. This leads to a potential tax time bomb since most retirees rely on these accounts as a primary source of income. Most of the money in these plans is contributed before tax, which means any withdrawals in your retirement years are going to be taxed as ordinary income.

Imagine you have $1 million in your 401(k) today. If you took out $100,000, the taxes you would pay today could be substantially lower than taxes you would have to pay in the future, should there be an increase in taxes. If there's a hike in future tax rates, that million-dollar 401(k) isn't as valuable as you thought it was when more of the account is going to Uncle Sam.

There are a few ways to help diversify the tax status of your accounts. The first is to consider a Roth IRA in combination with your 401(k), assuming you're under the income limits. If you're not eligible, you might be able to contribute to a Roth 401(k) or possibly even a **backdoor Roth IRA,** but it can be tricky. You should consult with a tax advisor when considering the backdoor option.

Roth IRAs provide tax-free growth and tax-free income, but to get money into this type of account, the taxes must be paid first. There are two primary ways to stash money into a Roth IRA: contributions and conversions.

Contributions are fairly straightforward. The government allows you to invest a small amount into these accounts on a year-to-year basis. **Roth conversions** allow you to take a pretax asset, like an IRA, and take a portion of that account and move it to a Roth IRA. We like to see the taxes paid from an outside source to maximize the conversion amount. You can do this at any time, but our preferred time is right after retirement, when your income is lower, and before you turn seventy-three and are forced to take distributions from your IRA.

Another option for tax diversification is life insurance. During your working years, it's wise to have life insurance to provide for your family in the event of your early passing.

Most people buy term insurance because it's the cheapest option; it isn't permanent and doesn't build cash value.

In some instances, it can make sense to explore a life insurance policy that builds a cash value, such as whole life or universal life. These vehicles can be complex, and they aren't right for every investor, but if you're a higher-income earner phased out of a Roth and looking for tax-free accumulation, this vehicle could be beneficial.

A life insurance policy that builds a cash value is a highly debated concept in the financial planning community, and it needs to be structured correctly to be effective. We've run into financial planners who call such policies a section 7702 plan, a **life insurance retirement plan (LIRP)**, a tax-free supplement strategy, or some other fancy term. The truth is these policies are just overfunded life insurance.

Under section 7702 of the tax code, life insurance can accumulate tax-deferred, and you're allowed to take tax-free loans from life insurance if set up properly. If you google "life insurance retirement plan" or "LIRP," you'll find articles that bash the concept and articles that praise it. It's another tool in the toolbox that may make sense for some, but for others it has no place in their retirement plan.

We tend to see LIRPs as more of a fit for high-income earners with a decade or more until their planned retirement date. The nice thing is that most high-income earners we meet already have a need for life insurance and are looking for a place to save extra dollars. Why not kill two birds with one stone and buy a policy that provides your heirs with a death benefit *and* supplements your 401(k) by being able to take tax-free loans from it? On top of that, LIRPs can also be structured to provide extra health care protection by allowing early access to the death benefit in the event of chronic or critical illness.

Just like the Roth, after-tax money is used to fund this strategy. There are real benefits to this strategy, but there are also some challenges. LIRPS tend to have high front-end costs, so you need to have a longer time horizon when implementing this strategy. Another challenge is finding an unbiased financial advisor who can help determine if there's a fit—an advisor who represents you and not a specific company. This is important because all kinds of different factors need to be tailored to your needs. The average insurance salesperson who represents a company may not be in a position to compare different strategies from multiple companies.

The moral of the story? Start thinking of ways to diversify your future tax burden, especially if the bulk of your money is tied up in pretax retirement plans. With the national debt over $34 trillion, there's no doubt that there's a target on the back of retirees and their pretax retirement plans. The time to start diversifying with these strategies is now, because there is a possibility of future legislative changes that could limit or even eliminate these strategies. The more you can pile into tax-free accumulation vehicles, the better off you'll be.

Three Key Takeaways

1. Retirees face five primary risks. To plan for a secure retirement, you must understand and mitigate the five primary risks: market risk, longevity risk, inflation risk, health care risk, and tax risk.

2. Longevity risk. Longevity risk refers to the unpredictability of how long an individual or couple will live. While increasing life expectancy is positive, it introduces financial planning challenges. Retirees who live longer may risk outliving their assets. Strategies like guaranteed lifetime income streams, including pensions and Social Security, can help mitigate this risk.

3. Inflation risk. Inflation erodes the purchasing power of your money over time, which can impact retirees significantly in the long term. It is critical to factor in inflation when planning for retirement, to diversify assets to combat inflation, and to consider investments like Treasury inflation-protected securities and short-term bond funds.

Questions for You

- How can you effectively plan for longevity risk, considering the three distinct phases of retirement (Go-Go, Slow-Go, and No-Go)? What financial strategies can help sustain you throughout these phases?
- What are the pros and cons of different methods for handling health care risk, such as long-term care insurance, self-insuring, and health care riders on annuities or life insurance policies? How should retirees assess their needs in this regard?
- What are some strategies for diversifying the tax status of retirement accounts?
- How can you best protect your savings from potential future tax increases or legislative changes?
- How does tax planning factor into overall retirement planning strategies?

Notes:

FIVE

The Key Element of a Successful Retirement Plan

A man who does not think and plan long ahead will find trouble right at his door.

—Confucius

Navigating the complexities of building a retirement plan can feel like charting a course through a sea of uncertainties. Life expectancy, market volatility, economic factors, and regulatory changes all contribute to the twists and turns your plan may encounter. These are what we refer to as known unknowns—factors we recognize as influential but cannot precisely predict. Amidst this maze of variables, however, lies a steadfast anchor within your control: self-discipline.

In his book, *The Science of Self-Discipline,* Peter Hollins offers invaluable insight, advocating for a powerful tool called the 10-10-10 Rule.[12] Before succumbing to impulses or temptations, Hollins suggests pausing to consider how your actions will impact you not just in the moment but also in the near and distant future—10 minutes, 10 hours, and

---

12 Peter Hollins, *The Science of Self-Discipline: The Willpower, Mental Tough-ness, and Self-Control to Resist Temptation and Achieve Your Goals (Live a Disciplined Life),* (CreateSpace Independent Publishing, 2017), 145–146.

10 days from now. This simple yet profound rule underscores the importance of thinking beyond immediate gratification and prioritizing the long-term consequences of your choices.

One area where self-discipline plays a crucial role in retirement planning is managing spending. Effectively controlling expenses, distinguishing between needs and wants, and adhering to a budget are essential components of financial discipline. By practicing disciplined spending habits, individuals can better align their resources with their long-term goals and mitigate the risk of financial strain in retirement.

Even more significant is the management of emotions in financial decision-making. Emotions such as fear, greed, and impulsiveness can cloud judgment and lead to irrational choices that undermine financial well-being. By cultivating emotional resilience and practicing mindfulness, individuals can make decisions based on reason rather than emotion, ensuring a more stable and secure financial future.

It may seem easy, but one of the toughest parts of retirement is figuring out your spending, keeping tabs on it, and creating a budget that lets you enjoy your golden years. Have you heard the rule of thumb that to plan a retirement budget all you need to plan for is 65–75 percent of your working years' income in retirement? We've found over the years that this advice is extremely unreliable. It all comes down to your goals in retirement. You're not going to wake up and watch Netflix all day (at least not every day). You're going to travel more, you're going to spend more on your grandkids, and you're going to pick up new hobbies. Every day is now a Saturday, and your expenses could easily increase in the early, golden years of your retirement.

In some cases, we do see clients' expenses drop off significantly in retirement, but mostly they either stay about the same or increase. A core element of putting together a sound retirement plan is knowing your budget down to the last dollar.

When we're developing a retirement income plan for our clients, we always ask, "What are your expenses?" They often reply with a blank stare and a smirk. They have no idea what their expenses are because they've always had income coming in and knew they were taken care of. Becoming a good budget tracker means breaking down your expenses into two categories: essential expenses and discretionary expenses.

Essential expenses are expenses you need to live your life: food, utilities, mortgage, health care, and transportation. These expenses might fluctuate slightly from month to month, but if you track these over a twelve-month period, you'll have a good idea of what you need per month to cover these costs. Don't wait to learn how to track your essential expenses until you retire.

The other half of your expenses, discretionary expenses, are more difficult to predict and to track. These expenses can vary from month to month, and they include things like vacations, home improvements, gifting, and charity. When building a retirement plan, it's important to think about what you want to do in retirement, set a budget, and stick to it. It's also important to factor in how these expenses might vary in retirement. Maybe your travel expenses will be higher for the first five years and then drop off dramatically once you've hit all your destinations and are sick of dealing with the airlines. Maybe your mortgage will fall off ten years into retirement. Maybe you're planning on downsizing your home. Maybe your life insurance is no longer needed or expires in a few years. These are all things that need to be factored into your monthly budget so you can build the best possible plan to enjoy your retirement years.

According to Experian, a data analytics and consumer credit reporting company, the average household led by a person age sixty-five or older spends $4,345 per month.[13] We agree with the average, but we have clients who far exceed this, and clients who keep their expenses under this mark. What type of retiree are you? If you fall under the "Hobby Becomes My Jobby" or "Travel the World" categories, you might find yourself meticulously planning your golf schedule or searching luxury cruise vacations, while other retirees are mastering the art of coupon clipping to stretch their retirement dollars as far as possible.

For some people, retirement is a budgeting ballet where early-bird specials and senior discounts take center stage; sometimes it's a dramatic decision on whether to splurge on the expensive artisanal cheese, or simply go with

---

13 Gayle Sato, "How Much Will You Spend in Retirement?" Experian, June 22, 2023, https://www.experian.com/blogs/ask-experian/how-much-will-you-spend-in-retirement/.

the discount cheddar. Retirement: Where you can simultaneously live your dreams and turn every grocery run into an episode of *The Price Is Right*.

Before you answer questions regarding extravagant vacations and fancy cheese, you should first answer the following questions:

- Is this expense within my budget?
- How will this purchase make you feel ten minutes, ten hours, ten days, and ten years from now?

If a client tells us they want to generate $5,000 a month of income from their portfolio, our job is to help them build a budget that fits that amount of income. But it's their job to make sure they stick to those expenses.

Many of our clients have a hard time understanding how to track their expenses and build a reasonable and achievable budget around those expenses. This shouldn't come as much of a surprise. Most of us aren't terribly skilled at building and following a budget when we're working, let alone planning to retire. There's too much life to manage in our working years. When money is coming in, we fail to look at how much we're spending versus how much we're making because we have other pressing issues to think about.

Going beyond the budget, we also find that in most families one spouse pays the bills while the other is unaware of what's going on with their finances, let alone their expenditures. Few couples sit down to discuss these details in their working years, and the same is true for their retirement. Many people take pride in overseeing the finances for their families, which can sometimes leave one spouse in the dark.

The financial industry has a term for people who manage their own investments: the **"do-it-yourselfer."** Are you a do-it-yourselfer? There's nothing wrong with that. Some people eat, sleep, and breathe this stuff in retirement, and they enjoy planning and providing for their family. We will, however, issue a word of caution: You're not Warren Buffet. We can tell you with almost 100 percent certainty that if you try to beat the market, you will eventually get burned.

Have you ever had an ache or pain or a bump or rash and searched the internet to self-diagnose? How did that work out? I think we're all guilty of this. The issue is minor, so you google it in hopes of finding a simple remedy. Two hours later you're fully immersed in article after article, convinced that your symptoms spell impending doom within the next six months. Finally, you make an appointment to see a professional. Sometimes you just need to seek out professional help. Whether it's your health or your wealth on the line, recognizing the value of a second opinion is crucial.

Some of the most interesting parts of our profession concern behavioral finance and the cognitive biases associated with managing your money. Being trained on the psychological side of investing allows us to recognize trends in investor behavior. After wonderful returns in 2020 and 2021, some investors were facing the behavioral problem of self-attribution bias, which leads to overconfidence. This can be dangerous.

For over a decade prior, the market had been on a historic bull run. Investors were starting to think they had the magic touch—anything they threw their money into was gaining value. We all want to think we have the Warren Buffet–like ability to outperform the market, but we don't. Think of it this way: If you're sailing with pleasant winds and calm, open waters, you're probably going to be fine. But a smooth sea never made a skilled sailor. On the financial side, you could say a bull market never made a skilled investor. Once you hit rough waters, your ability will be tested, and you might not be fine.

The cold, hard truth is humans make terrible investors. We can be emotional, irrational, moody, greedy, and fearful—all in one week, depending on what the market is doing. Acting irrationally can result in common investment mishaps like buying or selling at the exact wrong time. Most investors have a tough time separating emotion from their finances, which is why advisors have to play the role of a coach every now and then.

The excerpt below from DALBAR's Quantitative Analysis of Investor Behavior does a great job of addressing the psychological complexities of investing:

When discussing investor behavior it is helpful to first understand the specific thoughts and actions that lead to poor decision-making. Investor behavior is not simply buying and selling at the wrong time, it is the psychological traps, triggers and misconceptions that cause investors to act irrationally. That irrationality leads to buying and selling at the wrong time, which leads to underperformance.

There are 9 distinct behaviors that tend to plague investors based on their personal experiences and unique personalities.[14]

Investor Behavior

Loss Aversion
Anticipating high returns with low risk.

Narrow Framing
Making decisions without fully weighing all consequences.

Gambler's Fallacy
The belief that future outcomes are influenced by past events.

Confirmation Bias
The tendency to search for information that confirms one's preexisting beliefs.

Anchoring
Tethered to familiar experiences, even when they are unsuitable.

Herding
Replicating the actions of others despite encountering unfavorable results.

Regret
Placing greater emphasis on errors of action than on errors of inaction.

Mental Accounting
Taking excessive risk in one area while avoiding rational risk in another.

Illusion of Control
The belief that one has more control over outcomes than is actually the case.

---

14 2020 QAIB Report, Quantitative Analysis of Investor Behavior, Dalbar Inc., 2020.

These nine investor behaviors lead investors to fall prey to the seven deadly sins of investing, listed below:

1. **Stock Picking (Envy):**
   Stock picking involves coveting specific stocks that appear lucrative because someone else recommends them. This desire to replicate others' success can prompt investors to make decisions based on comparison rather than thorough analysis. Whether it's a tip from a neighbor, a recommendation from a blog, or a mention on a TV show, succumbing to the envy of others' perceived gains may lead investors astray from their own investment strategies. Always remember that for every **multi-bagger** stock someone brags about, they likely have multiple flops to go along with it.

2. **Market Timing (Greed):**
   Market timing stems from an insatiable desire for wealth and attempting to maximize gains by predicting short-term market movements, often fueled by a **fear of missing out (FOMO).** Market timing can involve getting out of the market attempting to time a market crash, or it could be taking a heavier allocation into equities to catch a bull run.

3. Overconfidence (Pride):

Past successes can lead to overconfidence, by assuming that what worked before will continue to bring success. In the casino, they call this the **house money effect**. After a few wins you might believe you have a special ability to pick winning stocks or time the market correctly, leading you to take on more risk than you can handle. Overconfidence can also lead investors to believe they can predict short-term market movements accurately. This belief may result in frequent buying and selling of investments, leading to higher transaction costs and tax inefficiencies.

4. Concentrated Stock (Gluttony):

By overindulging in one stock and allowing it to make up a significant portion of your portfolio, you are ignoring the benefits of diversification and exposing oneself to excessive risk. Many times, a stock becomes concentrated because it performs well, and would result in a taxable gain if the stock were to be sold. Incurring a tax bill is never fun, we get that, but sometimes it's critical to realize gains to maintain proper diversification. There are other strategies worth considering here, such as **covered calls, protective puts, donor advised funds,** and **charitable remainder trusts**.

5. Portfolio Drift (Sloth):

Like sloth, or laziness, neglecting the maintenance of a well-balanced portfolio can have adverse effects. Allowing a portfolio to drift without **rebalancing** may result in suboptimal performance and incremental risk drift. For instance, consider a 60/40 portfolio that isn't rebalanced; over time, it could gradually shift to a 65/35 or 70/30 model as equities outperform, inadvertently increasing the risk of the strategy.

6. Strategy Abandonment (Wrath):

Like wrath, reacting emotionally rather than thoughtfully can lead to detrimental financial consequences. When investors allow their emotions to dictate their actions, they may be inclined to abandon their investment strategies hastily. Investing is a long-term game and success cannot be measured on a short-term scale. The abandonment of a strategy is typically a knee-jerk reaction due to **recency bias**. Just as wrathful actions are often regretted later, abandoning a well-thought-out investment strategy can result in missed opportunities and potential losses.

7. Track Record Investing (Lust):

The desire for higher returns often draws people to what's made big gains before. This approach, often dubbed **track record investing**, means looking only at past performance without considering the bigger picture. But just because something did well before doesn't mean it will again. It's like chasing after something because it's been good in the past, without thinking about whether it will stay that way.

Associating these investor sins with the traditional Seven Deadly Sins emphasizes the behavioral and emotional aspects that can lead to poor investment decisions. Understanding and mitigating these tendencies can contribute to a more disciplined and successful investment strategy. Conversely, the seven virtues of investing stand as a counterbalance to these sins:

1. Patience: Waiting calmly for investments to grow over time without succumbing to impulsive decisions. Good things take time.
2. Diligence: Consistently putting in the effort to research and monitor investments to make informed decisions.
3. Temperance: Exercising restraint and moderation in investment decisions, avoiding excessive risk-taking or speculative behavior.
4. Humility: Acknowledging that investing involves uncertainties and being open to learning from both successes and failures.

5. **Charity:** Recognizing the importance of giving back and supporting charitable causes with a portion of investment profits. Consider **qualified charitable distributions** for those who have reached age 70.5.

6. **Self-Control:** Maintaining discipline in managing investments and resisting emotional impulses that may lead to irrational decisions.

7. **Freedom:** Using wealth to empower oneself and others, promoting personal and societal growth.

For the DIY investor, mastering self-discipline is paramount to steering clear of these pitfalls and adhering to the virtues of investing. It's about staying focused, making sound decisions, and sticking to your long-term goals, even when the market gets turbulent. So, whether you're managing your investments on your own or with the help of a financial advisor, focusing on self-discipline can make all the difference in your financial journey.

No two retirees are exactly alike, and in most cases they're wildly different. Everyone has different goals and their own set of assets with which to accomplish these goals. This is why it's important to hire a retirement planner who will get to know you and your family, the various goals you have for your retirement, and what assets you have to work with.

Step one is determining our clients' goals. Step two is helping them define the budget that meets those goals. Step three is organizing their assets and putting a plan in place to meet their budget, all while fostering self-discipline to stay on track with their financial objectives.

Retirement Trivia

What common behavioral bias, often leading to investor underperformance, describes the tendency of individuals to hold on to losing investments for too long and sell winning investments too quickly?

a. The Disposition Effect

b. Loss Aversion

c. Anchoring

d. The Gambler's Fallacy

The answer can be found on page 180.

Case Study

Jill was probably our most financially conservative client. Her husband, Pat, had been a do-it-yourselfer his whole life. He had built up a seven-figure portfolio and enjoyed managing it. He was old school and would call up his stockbrokers to make trades for him. He religiously watched Jim Cramer's *Mad Money* and subscribed to numerous research magazines.

In his seventies, Pat began to notice issues with his memory. His doctor told him he was showing early signs of dementia. Right then and there he decided to find a financial advisor Jill could trust. Jill was a novice when it came to anything financial and had no interest in learning about it. It wasn't even a month after his doctor's visit that Pat came into our office and organized his accounts from various companies.

A little over a year after becoming our client, Pat passed away. Fortunately, for Jill, Pat noticed his memory issues and established a relationship with us. In retirement planning, for a do-it-yourselfer, the risk of cognitive decline can be just as dangerous as the risks mentioned in the previous chapters. If Pat hadn't come to us, or ignored his memory issues, would Jill have found an advisor she was comfortable discussing her finances with? Would she have a reliable monthly income and a plan in place? Most of all would she have the peace of mind knowing that her husband took care of her and made sure she had a team that would continue to take care of her?

Pat did a tremendous job of getting them to where they were, and just as importantly, he helped create a plan that wouldn't leave Jill in the dark. Many spouses don't have the foresight to organize their finances and establish a relationship for the surviving spouse.

People like Pat and Jill come to us all the time. We break down their goals, and once we understand what our clients want out of their retirement, we build an income strategy that accomplishes their goals and matches up with the assets they have (pensions, portfolios, stocks, and savings).

Regardless of what you know, what you think you know, what you've been told on TV or in how-to books, or what friends and family have told you, your advisor must talk to you about different ways to protect your money, how to create income from your assets, and how to manage the various investment vehicles to meet your needs.

At our company, we take education seriously. Keeping up with the ever-changing financial industry is a job in and of itself. Whether it's reading new books, watching educational webinars, reading trade journals, or attending investment conferences, it's important an advisor keeps up-to-date on the latest developments in the financial markets. As **Certified Financial Planner**™ professionals, we are required to complete thirty hours of continuing education every two years, in addition to the twenty-four hours every two years required by the department of insurance. We're not tooting our own horn here. The point is that staying current on the markets and the evolving financial system is more than just a hobby—it's a career. It's something that may prove to be too difficult or stressful when you're trying to enjoy your nonworking years.

Whether it be managing your emotions or managing your spending, becoming a master of self-discipline is the key piece to solving the retirement puzzle. Once we have an accurate budget, we can then start adding pieces to build a retirement plan. When building this plan, your advisor shouldn't just be trying to sell you the newest mutual fund or annuity; they should be teaching you about all the various options that exist. There is no one-size-fits-all investment. There is no perfect investment. Every investment has a string attached, whether it's market volatility, a fee, a time commitment, or an interest rate risk. In the next chapter we'll discuss several investment options and the pros and cons of each.

Three Key Takeaways

1. Self-discipline is a fundamental trait that plays
    a crucial role in retirement planning success.
    It enables individuals to overcome challenges,
    pursue long-term goals, and maintain consistency
    and integrity in their actions and decisions.
2. Budgeting is crucial. The difficulty of
    understanding, tracking, and building a budget for
    retirement expenses is a significant challenge for
    retirees. You must distinguish between essential
    expenses (food and utilities) and discretionary
    expenses (vacations and gifts) and to plan for both.
3. Investment and behavioral challenges. The
    challenges of managing investments in
    retirement include the risk of cognitive decline,
    overconfidence, and emotional decision-making.
    It's important to seek professional financial advice.

Questions for You

- How might your goals impact your financial planning and budgeting?
- Do you have a clear understanding of your current expenses, including both essential and discretionary costs?
- Are you prepared to track and manage your expenses in retirement?
- Have you considered the potential cognitive and emotional challenges that could affect your investment decisions in retirement?
- Have you thought about the benefits of seeking professional financial advice to navigate these challenges?

Notes:

(SIX)
Common Mistakes to Be Aware Of

Every advantage has its disadvantage,
and every disadvantage has its advantage.

– John Wooden

You've built a retirement budget that fits your goals and provides for future expenses. The next step is to look deeper into your portfolio to ensure it isn't strapped with hidden fees that could be sapping your retirement. You've worked long and hard to build a portfolio that works for you and your family, but with all the hidden fees, you could be losing thousands of dollars (if not hundreds of thousands of dollars) over the lifespan of your retirement. While it's true that all financial planners need to make a living, there's no reason you can't find an advisor who puts your interests and security first. If you're not sure how your financial planner is making money by managing your finances, it might be time to find out.

Part One: Mutual Funds

Mutual funds are a common investment vehicle we see from prospective clients. They're the most common investment you'll find inside an employer-sponsored retirement plan, as they can maximize diversification with just a handful of funds. There are good funds and bad funds, and it can be tricky for an uninformed investor to know which is which. Investors might think they're diversified because they own twenty different mutual funds. More often than not, there is significant **correlation** between these funds because they own similar holdings inside the funds.

This is the first issue with mutual funds, referred to as *overlap* or *stock intersection*.

When you're saving for retirement, we generally recommend lower-cost index funds inside the plan, which track a major index such as the S&P 500 in a cost-efficient manner. This means there is little activity inside the fund (buying and selling different positions), keeping costs down. More active funds, however, are another story.

As a fund trades more and more, this is called *turnover*. You can find the **turnover rate** by googling the fund and doing a little bit of research. A 2009 study of thousands of US equity mutual funds discovered the trading costs for investors is an average 1.44 percent.[15] It's important to note that these additional trading costs are a result of turnover

---

15   Anna Prior, "The Hidden Costs of Mutual Funds," *The Wall Street Journal*, March 1, 2010, https://www.wsj.com/articles/SB100014240527487033829045 75059690954870722.

and are not reported in the expense ratios in your prospectus. So, it's up to investors to do extra research.

If you're investing in mutual funds in an after-tax account, this turnover can also cause tax inefficiencies when it comes to the fund distributing capital gains. Since this study, pressure has been placed on the mutual fund industry to become more transparent, and we've seen these costs become more reasonable.

Another issue with mutual funds is what is referred to as a *load*. If you own a mutual fund that is a share class known as A, B, or C, these come with additional costs to provide compensation to a broker. A-shares charge a commission up front, B-shares charge a commission on the back end, and C-shares tend to have higher annual costs. If your advisor is working in your best interest, you shouldn't see any A, B, or C shares in your portfolio. There are usually better, lower-cost funds available to invest in.

The last issue we see with mutual funds is recommendation bias. If you see a JP Morgan advisor, there's a better chance they'll recommend JP Morgan funds over different funds. Same for Oppenheimer. Same for T. Rowe Price. Same for American Funds. And so on. If you're seeing an advisor, this is another reason it's important to find an independent advisor who doesn't have a bias toward a grouping of funds.

Think of it like buying a car. If you go to a Ford dealership, what kind of car do you think they'll recommend? Not that there's anything wrong with Ford cars, but wouldn't it be nice if you could go to a dealership that represents all car makers? That's what an independent advisor can do for your portfolio.

What's the Alternative?

There's a place for passive management within a portfolio, but at our firm we also use separately managed accounts (SMAs) and unified managed accounts (UMAs). These accounts have been in a revolution in the financial industry over the past two decades, originally starting with large institutions but now available to individual investors. There are various minimums to SMAs and UMAs, but anyone with $250,000 would have access to an array of strategies.

This approach is complex and can be challenging for investors to grasp, so let's look at an example.

A portfolio manager named Bob is launching an equity strategy composed of fifty stocks. When launching, he decides to launch both a mutual fund and an SMA offering. From a client perspective, both the mutual fund and the SMA will look different on their statement. A statement holding the mutual fund will be simple: It will list the fund and the net asset value from the close of business on the statement's effective date. The SMA statement, however, will list each individual stock and their respective values separately (hence the term, separately managed account). While these investments are similar, there are key differences as well.

The first difference is the fee structures. The mutual fund may have a sales charge, in addition to its disclosed expense ratio, which includes the manager's fee, operating costs, and 12b-1 fees (marketing costs). The second difference is the hidden costs, or trading costs as a result of turnover. Naturally, funds with higher turnover will have higher hidden expenses because of the additional trading. The third and final difference is that mutual funds have another hidden cost, the cost of tax inefficiency. This is particularly hard to measure because it depends on the tax status of the money and the tax rate of the investor.

Let's say Bob bought Facebook stock in the first year of its availability, at $30 per share. Years later, let's say you bought into the mutual fund when Facebook was trading at $200 per share. If Bob decides to sell off the position of Facebook after it fell to $150, you get to share the tax burden of this capital gain, even though you saw a loss in the share price. In other words, you get hit with taxes on the gain, even though, overall, you took a loss. This is referred to as *phantom income.*

In an SMA, the fee structure is much more transparent. You pay a management fee, usually an annual fee ranging from 0.75 percent to 1.5 percent per year, depending on the complexity of the strategy. Please keep in mind, you don't want your broker or investment advisor to be incentivized to make changes in the accounts by receiving a commission on trades. This could result in unnecessary *churning* within your accounts.

In the above example Bob is selling off his investment in Facebook, and if your SMA is in an after-tax account, you get to use that loss to either offset other gains or deduct it on your tax return, rather than get hit with capital gains.

To take it a step further, let's say Bob never sold his Facebook stock. It's December, and you have realized $10,000 in capital gains from the sale of Apple stock. Assuming the capital gains tax rate is 15 percent, you would incur a $1,500 tax bill. A good financial advisor will look at the client's overall portfolio, see Facebook is down in value, and tax-loss harvest the position. This means we could sell off the Facebook stock at a loss and offset a portion of the gains. This is referred to as **tax-loss harvesting**.

When performing this maneuver, you want to reinvest in something similar in case of a market rebound. In this case you could buy a technology ETF, hold it for thirty days, and then sell it to buy back the Facebook stock. You don't want to immediately buy back Facebook though because of the wash-sale rule. The **wash-sale rule** means that if you sell a stock at a loss and buy it back before thirty days, the IRS won't allow you to take the loss. Imagine you realize a $5,000 loss as a result of selling the Facebook stock. You can offset the capital gain in Apple by $5,000. Now you've cut that tax bill of $1,500 in half.

In the industry we call this adding *annuitization, surrender charges,* to the portfolio (opposed to a *tax drag* with mutual funds). In layman's terms we call this *when life gives you lemons, make lemonade.*

Part Two: Annuities

No investment or insurance strategy is more polarizing than annuities.

Some financial professionals love them. Some hate them. And some claim to hate them—but only certain kinds, which is extremely confusing for the average investor.

Roger Ibbotson, PhD, professor in the practice emeritus of finance at Yale School of Management, recently completed a study back-testing equity, fixed income, and fixed indexed annuity combinations. He concluded that he is "not necessarily advocating you go all in," on fixed indexed annuities, but he thinks "combinations of stocks and bonds and fixed indexed annuities are good."[16]

And how about personal finance expert Suze Orman? If you've ever watched her TV show, you know that Suze is often emphatically against annuities, and for good reason. But she also recognizes that they can have a place in a retirement portfolio. Suze claims in her book *The Road to Wealth* that "if you don't want to take risk but still want to play the stock market, a good index annuity might be right for you."[17]

The single biggest mistake we see when it comes to annuities is seeing clients buy them as a stand-alone solution rather than as a component of an overall income plan.

---

16 Roger G. Ibbotson, *Fixed Indexed Annuities: Consider the Alternative*, Zebra Capital Management, January 2018, https://www.zebracapital.com/wp-content/uploads/2019/06/Fixed-Indexed-Annuities-Consider-the-Alternative-January-2018.pdf.

17 Suze Orman, *The Road to Wealth: A Comprehensive Guide to Your Money*, (Riverhead Books, 2001), 556.

Annuities are not a cure-all vehicle, but they may have a place in a properly constructed retirement plan along with equities and fixed income. Annuities can be a valuable tool if used properly and a real headache if used improperly.

There are two primary use cases for an annuity in a retirement portfolio. The first is safe growth. If you're buying an annuity expecting to match or exceed market returns, you'll likely be disappointed. It's no secret that a balanced retirement portfolio should consist of both equities and fixed income, with fixed income acting as the stable portion of the portfolio. In recent years, with fixed-income being highly volatile, certain annuity types may be viable alternative to provide the stabilization we're looking for with fixed-income, but come with their own pros and cons.

The second use case is guaranteed lifetime income. For those lacking pensions, or those in need of additional guaranteed income, an annuity can be a great way to protect yourself in the event you live longer than anticipated. It can also provide a tremendous benefit in delivering an uncorrelated income stream that isn't dependent on the stock or bond market.

Different Types of Annuities

Whenever our grandfather wanted to explain the differences in people, he would say, "That's why they make Chevys and Fords." There are at least as many different types of financial vehicles as there are motor vehicles from which to choose. This is often overwhelming.

Annuities aren't suitable for everyone. It comes down to personal choice—your circumstances, income, financial resources, objectives, tolerance for market risk, and investment timeline, which are all particular to you. There is no single cookie-cutter investment or retirement plan that is a perfect fit for all retirees. That's what makes investing so complex—trying to figure out the best solution to meet your specific needs.

An annuity is a vehicle you purchase from an insurance company. For the premium you pay, you receive certain fixed and/or variable growth options that are able to compound tax-deferred until withdrawn. When you're ready to receive income distributions, this vehicle offers guaranteed payout options through a process known as *annuitization*.

Most annuities have provisions that allow you to withdraw a percentage of earnings each year up to a certain limit. But withdrawals can reduce the value of the death benefit, and excess withdrawals above the restricted limit may incur **surrender charges** within the first three to ten years of the contract.

Because they're designed as a long-term retirement income vehicle, annuity withdrawals made before age fifty-nine-and-a-half are subject to a 10 percent penalty, and withdrawals may be subject to income taxes.

There are four types of annuities:
1. Deluxe model: **variable annuity**
2. Drive off the lot: **immediate annuity**
3. Safety rated: **fixed annuity**
4. Hybrid: **fixed indexed annuity**

Deluxe Model: Variable Annuity

A variable annuity consists of professionally managed portfolios that vary in both investment objectives and representative holdings. You may allocate your purchase payments across any number of these portfolios in whatever percentage you choose, with regard for your financial objectives and tolerance for market risk. Taxes on earnings from these portfolios aren't due until distributed, and you may transfer assets between portfolios without having to pay taxes on gains.

Professional money managers handle these various portfolios, so the fees you pay for each portfolio, combined with the overall administrative, mortality, and expense fees, can be quite high. Many variable annuities also offer optional riders guaranteeing minimum annual income for a specific number of years or even for life, available for an additional fee. Annuities with optional income riders tend to have fees commensurate with the additional risks, as underwritten by the issuing insurer.

When you factor in all the costs of variable annuities, they can easily reach (and even surpass) 3 percent on an annual basis.

Drive Off the Lot: Immediate Annuity

With an immediate annuity, you use a lump sum of money to purchase a contract from an insurance company in return for a guaranteed series of payouts. This stream of income is guaranteed for a specified period of time or for the rest of your (and even your spouse's) life—no matter how long you live.

The amount of the payout is based on several factors:

- How much money you use to buy the contract.
- The interest rate environment at the time you purchase the contract.
- The payout option and timing of your first payment.
- Your life expectancy, based on current age and gender.
- Any additional features you choose.

One thing to consider with an immediate annuity is that since there is no accumulation phase, you must annuitize immediately to receive income distributions. Once you annuitize with the life-only option, you forfeit access to your assets. When you die, your beneficiaries may be able to continue with a stream of income depending on the elected payout option, but the lump sum of money that could have been left to your heirs is forfeited to the insurance company.

Safety Rated: Fixed Annuity or Multi-Year Guaranteed Annuity

A fixed annuity or multi-year guaranteed annuity (MYGA) provides a guaranteed interest rate for a specific number of years to protect you from market fluctuations. Fixed annuities offer fixed interest rate periods over two, three, five, seven, or ten years—as well as annuitization payout options, including the option for guaranteed income for life.

The fixed annuity can help you conservatively accumulate assets to help cover fixed living expenses in retirement, but it doesn't offer substantial potential for growth. These annuities make for a great alternative to storing your cash in a savings account or CD.

Hybrid: Fixed Indexed Annuity

With a fixed indexed annuity (FIA), the contract issuer may credit your account value with a guaranteed minimum rate of return on your premium, plus the potential for additional gains linked to the performance of a specific market index, usually the S&P 500. At the end of each contract year, the insurance company measures the growth of the linked index over the previous twelve months and then credits your contract value with that growth, up to a predetermined cap. It may be an annual cap, a monthly cap, or a percentage of the growth of the index.

Because the FIA is linked to an unmanaged index, it tends to have lower administrative fees than a variable annuity. Some FIAs allow you to withdraw earnings without penalty up to a certain amount each year. But be aware that excess withdrawals may incur surrender fees and may also void the credit from the index-linked return.

An FIA's index-linked interest rate is computed based on one of three methods:

1. **Participation rate.** If the insurance company sets the participation rate at 40 percent, your fixed indexed annuity will be credited with 40 percent of the return rate experienced by the linked index.
2. **Spread/margin/asset fee.** This is the return rate of the linked index minus a percentage. For example, if the index gained 8 percent and the spread/margin/asset fee is 2 percent, then the annuity would be credited 6 percent.
3. **Interest rate cap.** Some FIAs allow you to benefit fully from index gains up to a specific percentage cap. This is the maximum growth percentage the annuity may earn.

An FIA is designed to work in any market environment. Whether the market is up, down, or flat, the fixed indexed annuity provides downside protection and the potential for gains linked to the performance of a market index.

As long as you abide by the terms of the contract, your principal is guaranteed against market loss from day one. Also, your interest gains lock in each year on your contract anniversary and cannot be taken away in a future market downturn.

Annuity Models in Simple Terms

A variable annuity is similar to mutual funds in that you have various investment options, referred to as *subaccounts*. Just like investing in a 401(k), you can choose to be aggressive, moderate, or conservative. Your account value benefits from the upside of the markets, but it is also vulnerable to market losses.

An immediate annuity is similar to a pension in that it gives you a payment for life (or a selected time period) and has no cash value to pass to your beneficiaries.

A fixed annuity is similar to a CD in that you give an insurance company a lump sum of money, and they offer you a fixed rate of return over the agreed-upon time period.

An FIA or hybrid annuity is similar to fixed income in that it provides a safer, more stable growth rate compared to the at-risk portion of your portfolio.

Annuity riders can also be added to the above contracts to enhance or tailor the features of the contracts. These riders can vary from providing guaranteed income without the need to annuitize right away, enhance the death benefit, or add health care features. Typically, these riders come with an additional cost commensurate with the benefit they are providing. For example, it is common for income riders to cost around one percent of the account value on an annual basis, but if your goal is to create a lifetime pension through an annuity, the one percent may be a cost you're willing to pay. For those looking to add a health care benefit, some companies allow the income payments to be doubled in the event of a long-term care event. This is typically triggered when the annuitant is unable to complete two of the six activities of daily living (eating, toileting, transferring, walking, bathing, and maintaining continence).

Please note: Annuity product guarantees rely on the financial strength and claims-paying ability of the issuing insurance company.

Retirement Trivia:

Placing an annuity in an after-tax account offers the significant advantage of deferring taxes on gains until withdrawal. However, what potential drawbacks might arise from this arrangement?

a. Gains are taxed as **ordinary income** when withdrawing.

b. Gains are withdrawn last.

c. Gains are tax-free after RMD age.

The answer can be found on page 181.

Three Key Takeaways

1. Hidden fees in your portfolio: It's important to recognize the importance of transparency in your holdings and understand the true cost of ownership of your funds. Be aware of the annual costs, possible front-end costs, and possible backend costs to get out of the vehicle.

2. Annuities in retirement planning: Approach annuities as part of a comprehensive retirement plan, rather than a standalone solution. Understand the fee structure and potential drawbacks associated with each type of annuity. As with any financial vehicle, make sure they are right for you.

3. Riders on annuities: If you are purchasing an annuity, riders allow you to customize the annuity to meet your needs. It is important to understand the costs/benefits of these riders.

Questions for You

- Have you checked your mutual funds for overlap or stock intersection to ensure you're truly diversified?
- Do you know the turnover rate of the mutual funds you're invested in and how it affects your costs?
- Are there any A, B, or C shares in your mutual fund portfolio, and if so, have you considered switching to lower-cost options? Which type of annuity (variable, immediate, fixed, or fixed indexed) aligns best with your retirement goals and risk tolerance?
- Have you explored the option of adding riders to your annuity contracts to tailor the features to your specific needs, and are you aware of the additional costs associated with these riders?

Notes:

(SEVEN)
How to Generate a Lifetime of Income in Retirement

Know what you own, and know why you own it.

– Peter Lynch

When running a retirement planning firm and building all sorts of plans, one thing you learn is that every retiree is different. Everyone who walks through our doors is in a unique financial position with unique goals. Not one single approach or tool is going to fit every single person.

We like to compare retirement planning to golfing. You don't use a driver for every shot; instead, you have multiple clubs in your bag to get you through the round in the best possible position. Similarly, you don't use one approach when investing; instead, you have multiple individual investment vehicles that work together to get in the best possible position to achieve a desired outcome. There's no one-size-fits-all, surefire vehicle you can throw your money into, call it a day, and yell, "Fore!"

The number one consistent concern for any retiree is generating enough income to pay for the rest of their lives.

Nearly two-thirds of baby boomers fear running out of money in retirement more than they fear death. This means we need to identify the assets in the portfolio that are going to be used for future income and allocate them in such a way that will preserve capital and generate that income.

Our father always says, "Hope for the best and plan for the worst." We've heard this quote over and over again, through every stage of life, whether it pertained to school, sports, or a new relationship. It never applies more than when it comes to creating retirement plans. What do we mean? Hope for a year where the S&P 500 goes up 20 percent, but plan for the bad years—you'll see many of them throughout your retirement.

As in golf, no matter what you do or how good a plan you have, everyone eventually ends up in a sand trap and has to pull out their trusty sand wedge to get back on course. A good retirement plan works the same way. You avoid risk, you plan for the future, and you play conservatively so that when something unexpected comes up, you have the tools to remedy the situation and get back on track.

Generating income from your portfolio is the most essential element to enjoying retirement. Every now and then we have a client who needs no income from their portfolio, but that's rare. Generating income from your portfolio is almost always necessary and should be one of your primary goals in retirement.

But how much can you safely take out on a year-to-year basis?

The 4 percent rule is a common rule of thumb used to determine the amount of funds to withdraw from a portfolio each year. The goal is to provide a steady stream of funds to the retiree while also keeping an account balance that will allow funds to be withdrawn for a number of years. The 4 percent rule has traditionally been thought of as a "safe" withdrawal rate, with adjustments for inflation as needed. There have been a number of studies in recent years that have looked into how this philosophy and other retirement income strategies stack up.

In a 2013 interview with Morningstar, David Blanchett, CFA, was asked the question if the 4 percent withdrawal rule can be depended upon in a low interest rate environment. His response was:

> A metric that we use in retirement-income research is the probability of failure, and that's how many times over a simulation your outcome fails. How many times can you achieve your goal of taking out 4 percent in year one, adjusted for inflation for thirty years? The 4 percent rule, as it is called, had about a 10 percent chance of failure, which is pretty good. But using yields today, it's more like 50 percent. And so the safety of that 4 percent strategy is very much open to question. So, what we found kind of in our research was that 3 percent is a better kind of starting place for retirees right now.[18]

18   Christine Benz and David Blanchett, "Time for the 3% Withdrawal Rule?" Morningstar, February 8, 2013, https://www.morningstar.com/articles/582877/time-for-the-3-withdrawal-rule.

Retirement researcher Wade Pfau, PhD and CFA, states in his book *How Much Can I Spend in Retirement?* that a safe withdrawal rate is unknown and unknowable.[19] Because we don't know what the future holds. Will the United States continue its superior market growth? Will bond yields stay return to historical lows we saw throughout the 2010s? Will we have a recession in the early years of retirement? How many years of retirement are we planning for?

There are so many unknown variables that go into retirement planning, so determining a safe withdrawal rate is impossible.

Pfau also states in his book that "individuals are the most vulnerable when their wealth is likely the largest it has ever been."[20] He explains how it may make sense to take a more conservative approach in your early years of retirement, whether it be with a bond strategy or income annuity. This reduces the sequence of returns or luck-of-the-draw risk, which is the leading cause of failure of the 4 percent rule.

We couldn't agree more.

A successful retirement plan always starts with identifying the core of the portfolio—the piece that's going to generate the essential monthly income you rely on, regardless of market conditions.

There are different investment tools with varying levels of risk. A retirement planner's job, first and foremost, is to educate their clients on these tools. Our job is to make our

---

19   Wade D. Pfau, *How Much Can I Spend in Retirement?: A Guide to Investment-Based Retirement Income Strategies*, (Retirement Researcher Media, 2017), 16.
20   Pfau, *How Much*, 60.

clients aware that because their goals are changing as they enter retirement, their asset allocation and risk level needs to change as well.

Asset allocation involves dividing an investment portfolio among different asset classes. The process of determining which mix of assets to hold in your portfolio is a highly personal one. The asset allocation that works best for you at any given point in your life will depend largely on your time horizon and your ability to take on risk.

Risk and reward are inextricably entwined when it comes to investing. The expression "no pain, no gain" may have originated in the athletic community, but it also describes the relationship between risk and reward. We can tell you from personal experience that running until you can't run another step, and then pushing for one more block, or one more tenth of a mile, is the way to train the body for the rigors of a foot race. We can also tell you from personal experience that every investment involves some degree of risk. Don't let anyone tell you otherwise. If you intend to purchase securities—such as stocks, bonds, or mutual funds—it is essential that you understand the risk (the pain) before you invest (and reap the gains).

The reward for taking on risk is the potential for a greater investment return. If you have a financial goal with a longer time horizon, you're likely to make more money by carefully investing in asset categories with greater risk, like stocks, rather than restricting your investments to assets with less risk, like bonds, CDs, and fixed annuities. On the other hand, investing solely in safe investments may be appropriate for short-term financial goals.

A vast array of investment vehicles exist: stocks and stock mutual funds, real estate, corporate and municipal bonds, bond mutual funds, target date funds, exchange-traded funds (ETFs), money market funds, and US Treasury securities. For many financial goals, investing in a mix of stocks and bonds can be an appropriate strategy.

Let's take a closer look at the characteristics of the three major asset categories: stocks, bonds, and cash equivalents.

Stocks

Stocks have historically had the greatest risk and highest returns among the three major asset categories. As an asset category, stocks are a portfolio's "heavy hitter," offering the greatest potential for growth. Stocks hit home runs, but they also strike out. The volatility of stocks makes them a risky investment in the short term. Since 2000, large cap US stocks as a group, for example, have lost money on average about one out of every four years. Sometimes the losses have been quite dramatic, but investors willing to ride out the volatile returns of stocks over long periods of time are generally rewarded with strong, positive returns.

When buying stocks or a basket of stocks such as an ETF or mutual fund, it's important to diversify through your domestic—and international—asset classes and sectors. History has shown that domestic and international stocks have moved in a cycle of alternating performance over the past forty years.

The Hartford Funds study "A Reboot for International Equities" researched rolling five-year returns for international and US equities since the mid-1970s.[21] The study observed multiple periods of US outperformance, followed by periods of international outperformance, and then returning to US outperformance again. Since 2011, the US has been in its strongest period of outperformance, as it has outperformed now for over thirteen years, eclipsing the 1991-2003 run. History would suggest, at some point, we will see a return to international outperformance.

Bonds

Bonds are generally less volatile than stocks but offer more modest returns. According to Morningstar, the **standard deviation** of US Large Cap Growth stocks is 21.82 percent, while US Investment Grade Bonds are nearly one-third the volatility at 7.08 percent.[22] As a result, investors approaching a financial goal might increase their bond holdings relative to their stock holdings. The reduced risk of holding more bonds would be attractive to investors, despite the lower potential for growth, because the goal is within reach. Keep in mind, certain categories like high yield bonds higher

21 Ralph Wakerly, "Asset Class Mean Reversion: 2024 Review and Outlook," Seeking Alpha, January 15, 2024, https://seekingalpha.com/article/4662834-asset-class-mean-reversion-2024-review-and-outlook.
22 "What Asset Allocation Return and Standard Deviation Assumptions Do You Use for Plans?" Morningstar Office, https://awgmain.morningstar.com/web-help/FAQs/What_assumptions_goalplans.htm.

returns,, but also carry a higher risk. We will expand on the risks of bonds later in this chapter.

Cash

Cash and cash equivalents—such as savings deposits, CDs, Treasury bills, and money markets—are the safest investments but offer the lowest return of the three key asset categories. The chances of losing money on an investment in this asset category are extremely low. The federal government guarantees many investments in cash equivalents. Investment losses in nonguaranteed cash equivalents do occur, but infrequently.

Retirement Trivia

When assessing portfolio volatility, standard deviation provides a confidence interval indicating that returns will typically fall within a certain range about 95 percent of the time. Consequently, approximately 5 percent of the time, returns may deviate beyond this range—specifically, 2.5 percent of the time, returns might be worse than anticipated, while 2.5 percent of the time, returns could exceed expectations. What term is commonly used to describe this phenomenon?

    a.   Volatility Anomaly

    b.   Deviation Paradox

    c.   Market Aberration

    d.   Tail Risk

The answer can be found on page 182.

Are Stocks Safer than Cash?

In the short-term, the primary benefit for cash is its safety. At the time of writing this book, money markets and CDs were paying in the 5 percent range. The downside with cash is that this 5 percent is taxed as ordinary income, not leaving you much growth beyond inflation on an after-tax basis.

But what about the long-term? In this case, the downside with cash is opportunity cost. The visualization below is from Brian Feroldi, a well-respected author with a gift for simplifying financial concepts.[23]

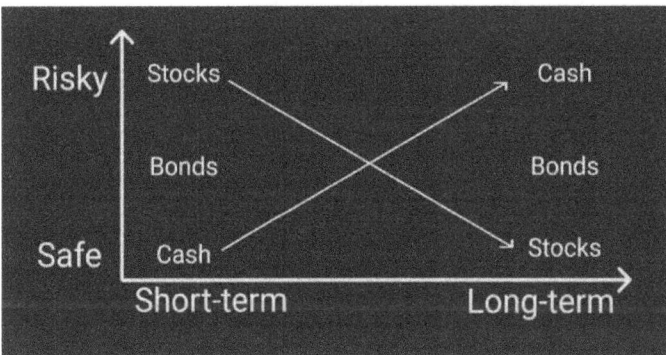

Short-term outlooks paint stocks as undeniably riskier than cash, Projecting the trajectory of the equity market over the next twelve to eighteen months is uncertain due to the high volatility of stocks, rendering attempts to time the market futile. However, the narrative shifts over time as stocks present a higher than expected return and better shield against inflation. Not to mention, stocks are more tax

---

23   Brian Feroldi, *99 Powerful Financial Lessons Visualized*, https://brianferoldi. ck.page/99.

efficient as you can defer the gains by not selling the stock or ETF, and qualified dividends/long-term capital gains are typically taxed at a more favorable rate.

The Traditional 60/40 Approach

The traditional approach to retirement planning is allocating 60 percent to equities and 40 percent to fixed income. Keep in mind, when using this strategy we always recommend keeping at least six months of expenses in cash. As we've previously mentioned in this book, this simple 60/40 allocation has worked wonders over the years.

Let's look at the last few decades in stocks: The 1980s and 1990s saw one of the longest economic expansions in US history. A trained monkey could pick a winner. In 1999, when the market knew only one direction—up—a six-year-old chimpanzee by the name of Raven chose her portfolio by throwing darts at a list of 133 internet companies. The whiz-kid chimp delivered a 213 percent gain, better than most of the pros on Wall Street. If Raven had been employed at a mutual fund company, she would have been ranked as the 22nd best money manager in the country—outperforming more than 6,000 of her competitors.[24]

Many who came of age as investors during that period expected the market to continue growing forever and have continued to invest like it's 1999.

---

24 "Most Successful Chimpanzee on Wall Street," Guinness World Records, https://www.guinnessworldrecords.com/world-records/most-successful-chim-panzee-on-wall-street.

Then the lost decade happened. From 2000 to 2009, we saw two recessions, and the S&P 500 provided negative returns over the whole decade. You might be thinking that if you had regularly put money into a 60 percent stock / 40 percent bond portfolio during the 2000–2010 decade, you would have had about a 4 percent return, and what's wrong with that?

Let's look at how you earned that 4 percent. You lost 30 percent. The market bounced back. You lost 40 percent. The market bounced back again. Meanwhile, the compound rate of return was 4 percent, but most investors didn't wait for the dust to settle and bought and sold at the wrong time. After they lost the first 30 percent, they went into sell mode and reduced their holdings. As a result, when the market started to recover, they only got part of the way back. While some people made that 4 percent, the average investor didn't get anywhere close to that.

As we stated before, humans can make for terrible investors. We're emotional, which causes us to become irrational, which causes us to make investing mistakes. The graph below, a 2023 Morningstar study, demonstrates this perfectly.[25]

---

25 "Mind the Gap 2023: A Report on Investor Returns in the United States," Morningstar, July 31, 2023, https://www.morningstar.com/lp/mind-the-gap.

Exhibit 1   The Gap by U.S. Category Group (10-Year Returns)

U.S. Category Group	Investor Return %	Total Return %	Gap
Allocation	5.98	6.44	-0.46
Alternative	-0.92	0.96	-1.88
International Equity	3.30	4.89	1.59
Municipal Bond	0.52	1.89	-1.37
Nontraditional Equity	2.10	4.16	-2.06
Sector Equity	6.42	10.80	-4.38
Taxable Bond	0.20	1.57	-1.36
U.S. Equity	10.99	11.77	-0.79
Overall	6.04	7.71	-1.68

Source: Morningstar Direct. Data as of Dec. 31, 2022. Excludes commodities category group. Gap numbers may not match differences in returns because of rounding.

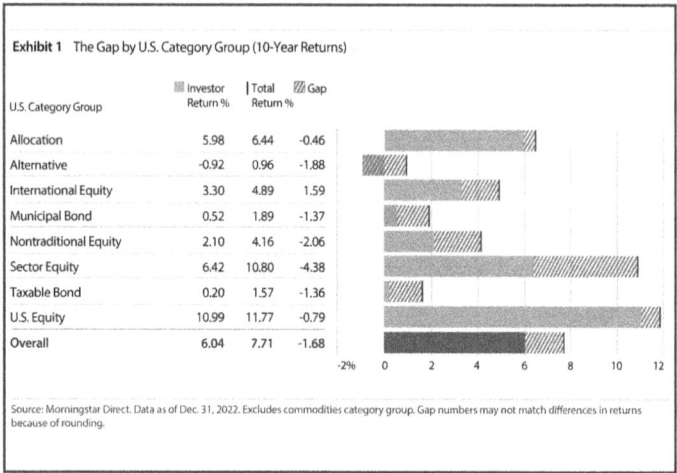

As you can see, the average investor underperforms in both equities and fixed income. Indexing has been a great way for investors to capture more equity returns, but as seen on this chart, not a great way to capture bond returns. Investors over the last decade only captured less than half the upside on bond funds.

Why is this? Perhaps investors don't know what types of fixed income to invest in. Or maybe they jump in and out at the wrong times, because fixed income can look rather boring when the market is roaring.

If the average taxable bond investor achieved a 0.20 percent return, compared to 1.57 percent, how would this impact a retirement investor who has 40 percent allocated to fixed income?

Prior to 2022 and 2023, we hadn't seen a significant rising interest rate environment in a few decades. And boy, was 2022–2023 significant. With inflation coming in hot off the COVID-19 pandemic, we saw the Fed rapidly increase rates 5 percent in less than two years' time. This was a black swan event for bonds, and it crushed any 60/40 investor.

According to Morningstar, here are the maximum drawdowns for two of the most popular fixed income ETFs:

- From 12/1/2021 to 10/31/2023, the iShares 20+ Year Treasury Bond was down -42.05 percent.[26]
- From 8/1/2021 to 10/31/2022, the iShares Core US Aggregate Bond was down -16.94 percent.[27]

What does this tell us?

It tells us that there are risks associated with bonds.

It tells us that longer-term bonds can drop catastrophically in a rising rate environment.

It tells us that fixed income, which is meant to be a safe haven to your portfolio, can provide negative returns over a whole decade when the effects of inflation are factored in.

Don't forget that the typical investor jumps in and out of the various markets at the wrong times, which means the numbers are sure to get worse. The main takeaway for today's retirees and pre-retirees, is that we may need to rethink the approach to the traditional retirement portfolio.

As investors, what do we do?

---

26 https://www.morningstar.com/etfs/xnas/tlt/risk.
27 https://www.morningstar.com/etfs/arcx/agg/risk.

This is a tough question, because no advisor in their right mind would say to jump out of bonds entirely. There are a couple of options that we like to see implemented.

First and foremost, you should be managing duration. Mismanaging duration is how we saw bank blowups in March 2023. Banks invested in long duration bonds to maximize their yield in the low-rate environment, not expecting the Fed to hike so rapidly. As we illustrated with the prior stated returns, many banks were sitting on large losses, rendering them insolvent. To prevent additional blowups, the Fed enacted the Bank Term Funding Program to loan banks money at par value for bonds majorly down in value. The program absorbed losses on bonds for banks and helped solve the crisis.

But as individuals, our friends at the Fed surely won't make us whole; we must face our consequences. So, if you're an investor down over 40 percent on a long-term Treasury, well, your best option is likely to hold it and hope it recovers sooner rather than later. But as an investor, if you were to properly manage the risk of your bond exposure, you likely wouldn't be in this predicament.

Before you go about managing **duration**, you need to understand what it is and how it works. Short-term fixed income will have a shorter duration. Longer-term fixed income will have a longer duration. A 1 percent move in interest rates will expect to move the price of the bond by its duration, in an inverse action, like a teeter-totter, as seen below.

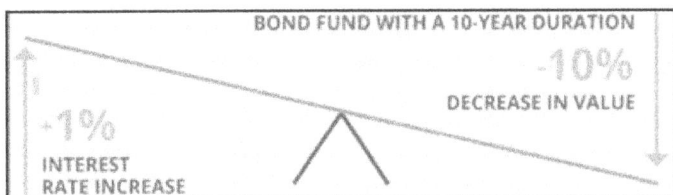

Keeping it simple, a 1 percent increase in rates would be expected to negatively impact the price of a ten-year duration bond by approximately -10 percent. Conversely, a 1 percent drop in rates would increase the value of the bond by approximately +10 percent. Now say the duration of the bond or bond fund is 1. That means a 1 percent increase or decrease in rates would only move it 1 percent up or down, making it a much more conservative investment.

Thinking back to 2020, the Fed dropped rates to zero, allowing for a wonderful year in fixed income. A smart move would have been to reduce duration to protect yourself from inevitable moves up in interest rates.

Now you may ask yourself, as you begin your journey into retirement, are bonds worth having a 40 percent allocation to? Is the juice worth the squeeze?

Now, it's easy to look at the negative real return on US Aggregate Bond Index over the last five years and decide to eliminate bond exposure altogether. But that's probably not the wisest move. After surviving the storm in fixed-income, now is not the time to jump ship. But it's certainly worth exploring bond alternatives.

We briefly discussed annuities in the previous chapter. fixed indexed annuities (FIAs) and multi-year guarantee annuities (MYGAs) can be solid replacements as bond alternatives. You can achieve similar modest returns in fixed income, while eliminating downside exposure. As we write this book, MYGA rates are hovering in the 5-6 percent range, and indexed annuity rates are higher than we've ever seen. FIA rates will adjust depending on the interest rate environment and volatility, so in times of higher interest rates, you would get an annuity with more upside capture.

The following chart illustrates the hypothetical potential of using FIAs as the financial tool to balance out the risk of bonds in a portfolio. Shown are the annual and ten-year average returns for some of the most common asset classes and portfolio mixes. If we look at simple diversification, combining two asset classes in a 60/40 example, which is common for a lot of retirees, we see that a 60/40 bond/stocks mix showed an average return of 6.1 percent. A 60/40 allocation featuring an FIA with crediting interest based on the performance of the S&P 500 with a 10 percent cap (60 percent) and large cap stocks (40 percent) had an average return of 9.4 percent.

	2013	2014	2015
Large Cap Equities	32.2%	13.5%	1.2%
Small Cap Equities	41.0%	6.2%	-1.8%
40/60 FIA/Stocks	23.3%	12.3%	0.8%
60/40 FIA/Stocks	18.9%	11.6%	0.6%
40/60 Bonds/Stocks	18.8%	10.4%	1.4%
10% S&P Cap	10.0%	10.0%	0.0%
Real Estate	2.3%	30.0%	2.4%
60/40 Bonds/Stocks	12.0%	8.9%	1.4%
International Equities	30.2%	-2.8%	8.6%
Bonds	-1.4%	5.8%	1.5%
Commodities	-1.8%	-33.0%	-34.1%

	2016	2017	2018
Large Cap Equities	11.8%	21.7%	-4.5%
Small Cap Equities	25.7%	13.1%	-8.6%
40/60 FIA/Stocks	11.0%	17.7%	-3.1%
60/40 FIA/Stocks	10.6%	15.4%	-2.2%
40/60 Bonds/Stocks	8.6%	14.7%	-3.0%
10% S&P Cap	9.5%	10.0%	0.0%
Real Estate	8.6%	4.9%	-6.0%
60/40 Bonds/Stocks	7.0%	11.2%	-2.2%
International Equities	-1.8%	38.9%	-23.0%
Bonds	3.8%	4.2%	-0.6%
Commodities	10.1%	3.9%	-13.9%

	2019	2020	2021	2022
Large Cap Equities	31.3%	18.2%	28.5%	-18.2%
Small Cap Equities	23.3%	11.1%	27.1%	-16.2%
40/60 FIA/Stocks	24.3%	15.8%	23.4%	-13.7%
60/40 FIA/Stocks	20.1%	14.3%	19.9%	-10.5%
40/60 Bonds/Stocks	23.0%	15.1%	16.6%	-16.5%
10% S&P Cap	10.0%	10.0%	10.0%	0.0%
Real Estate	28.9%	-4.6%	40.5%	-26.3%
60/40 Bonds/Stocks	18.8%	13.5%	10.7%	-15.6%
International Equities	21.9%	15.1%	9.5%	-27.6%
Bonds	10.4%	10.3%	-1.2%	-13.9%
Commodities	15.6%	-23.9%	38.8%	24.1%

	Annualized
Large Cap Equities	12.4%
Small Cap Equities	10.8%
40/60 FIA/Stocks	10.5%
60/40 FIA/Stocks	9.4%
40/60 Bonds/Stocks	8.3%
10% S&P Cap	6.9%
Real Estate	6.4%
60/40 Bonds/Stocks	6.1%
International Equities	4.9%
Bonds	1.7%
Commodities	-4.3%

This is just one example, using one type of annuity with a specific crediting strategy. It is provided not as a recommendation but as an illustration of the potential role an annuity can play in an overall retirement portfolio.[28]

We wish we could tell you there is a one-size-fits-all allocation that will outperform a traditional 60/40 portfolio in every environment, but there isn't. The key here is managing risk while seeking alternatives to fixed income when appropriate.

Does this mean you need to sell your bonds and buy an annuity?

No.

Fixed income is still valuable. It provides liquidity, stable income, and an uncorrelated return compared to the market.

If the average fixed-income investor achieved a return of just 0.2 percent annualized from 2013-2022. By

---

28 The 10 percent S&P Cap refers to a fixed indexed annuity tracking the S&P 500 Index with an annual cap of 10 percent. Note that the FIA does not participate directly in the index, but the S&P 500 is used as a reference to calculate interest credits. Provided for informational purposes only. The purpose of this presentation is to help explain how investment and insurance products can be designed to address financial needs and objectives in retirement. This is not intended and should not be interpreted as a presentation to help determine which securities or insurance products to buy or sell, nor shall it constitute an offer to sell or solicit or to buy a security or annuity. This information should not be used as the sole basis for making financial decisions. The source for returns for securities products is Yahoo Finance, using the following as representation of asset classes: Large Cap Equities = VFINX, Small Cap Equities = VTMSX, International Equities = VINEX, Real Estate = VNQ, Commodities = GSC, Index Bonds = VFICX and do not reflect actual trading. Source for 10 percent S&P 500 Cap is Yahoo Finance (S&P 500 Index). All investments are subject to risk, including the potential loss of principal. No investment strategy can guarantee a profit or protect against loss in periods of declining values. Any references to guarantees or lifetime income generally refer to fixed insurance products, never securities or investment products. Insurance and annuity product guarantees are backed by the financial strength and claims-paying ability of the issuing insurance company. Past performance is not a guarantee of future results.

incorporating an FIA as a fixed income alternative, you're reducing the human element of emotional investing, such as buying and selling at the wrong times. The liquidity restrictions and time commitments of fixed indexed annuities help to reduce the chances of emotional investing.

Here's the bottom-line: Annuities are complex vehicles that are right for some and wrong for others. Being a firm that works in both the investment management and annuity worlds, we can shed some light on this much-debated topic.

People's opinions and views vary in all aspects of life. It's no different when it comes to investments. Some may enjoy the thrill of taking risks in their portfolio and cashing in when they're right. We have a lot of clients who are risk-takers and scoff at the idea of having a conservative portfolio. Then we have clients who don't want to lose a dime of what they've worked so hard to build over their lifetimes and scoff at the idea of taking any risk. No matter what the risk profile is, in almost all cases, the client will need to generate income. So how do we do that with varying risk tolerances?

As advisors, it's our job to build a plan around that specific client's risk profile and income needs. The risk-taker client might have a portfolio made up entirely of stocks and bonds. We would look to kick up the yield of the portfolio and generate income through dividends and bond interest.

The risk-averse client still needs to generate income but is looking for less volatility. We may look to lean more heavily on bonds and pair that with a fixed indexed annuity to match the risk profile they want while still generating the income they need.

We can't say this enough: Annuities are just another tool in the toolbox, right for some and wrong for others. Our recommendation is to have your advisor build a plan with and without one. Know what that plan would look like both ways and educate yourself on your options so you can make the right decision for you, your spouse, and your family.

The trick is to find an advisor who understands retirement planning and can craft a plan according to your finances, your goals, and your life. You don't want to be sold a cookie-cutter plan or a silver bullet that doesn't exist. If you don't understand the various vehicles you have invested in, or if you fear certain investments you've heard bad things about, find a financial planner who can break these vehicles down for you and can craft a plan specifically for you that you are comfortable with.

Three Key Takeaways

1. Customized retirement planning. Every retiree has personal financial circumstances and goals, and there is no one-size-fits-all approach to retirement planning. Just as golfers use different clubs for different shots, retirement planning involves selecting individual investment vehicles tailored to your specific needs.

2. Income generation is key. A common concern for retirees is generating income to sustain their retirement lifestyle. It is important to identify and allocate assets for future income while preserving capital.

3. Diverse asset allocation. Asset allocation is fundamental to retirement planning. It involves dividing your investment portfolio among various asset classes to manage risk and return. Stocks, bonds, cash equivalents, and alternative assets all play a role in a diversified portfolio.

Questions for You

- What are your primary financial goals in retirement?
- How do your goals influence your choice of investment vehicles and asset allocation strategies?
- Have you received personalized retirement planning advice that takes into account your financial situation, or have you primarily relied on generic advice and investment vehicles that may not align with your specific needs and goals?
- How do you view annuities? Are you open to considering them as a potential component of your retirement income plan?

Notes:

(EIGHT)

Build a Retirement Plan
You Can Understand

Complexity is the enemy of execution.

– Tony Robbins

The last thing we want to hear from clients or prospective clients is "I've got all this money, and I still can't sleep at night" or "This isn't what I want for my retirement. I'm sick of riding the stock market roller coaster." Unfortunately, these sentiments are all too common in our industry. It can be easy to become stressed or anxious over your investments despite being in a great financial position. Often, this stems from a lack of a clear plan, or a plan that's simply too complex to grasp.

In the 1960s aircraft engineer Kelly Johnson of the US Navy coined the phrase "Keep it simple, stupid" (KISS). The KISS principle proposes that most systems work best if they're kept simple rather than complicated; therefore, simplicity should be a key goal in design. Unnecessary complexity should be avoided. We try to keep complex financial planning simple so that everyone can understand it—a task much harder than you would think. Keep in mind, our clients range from teachers to engineers to police officers, all with different financial backgrounds and knowledge. Some want to know every nitty-gritty detail of the plan; some want to know the basics.

Gone are the days when we inundated our clients with convoluted, hundred-page financial plans that left them overwhelmed and confused. Client feedback told us that such complexity was actually counterproductive, with one of our clients telling us "I'd like to know the engine works, but I don't need to know how it is built." So we decided to simplify our process and unexpectedly found inspiration by a visit to a kindergarten classroom.

We stopped by Steve's wife's kindergarten classroom to drop off some cupcakes for her birthday. Little did we know the cupcakes would turn the kids into sugar-crazed monsters, and the room was soon in chaos. Michelle stood at the front of the room and asked, "Who wants to play Red Light, Green Light?" All the kids lined up in an orderly fashion. When Michelle said "green light," the children walked toward her. When she said "red light," they stopped. The children who moved after she said "red light" were eliminated; the first child to make it to the front won.

On our way back to the office, we conceptualized the idea of red money and green money (and yellow money). It became our way of explaining to clients how they can allocate their money.

Green Money

Green money embodies the bedrock of financial security. It's the money you need to survive, the money you must protect to take care of your finances and essential expenses (mortgage, utilities, food, prescriptions, and other basic necessities). We consider green money to be liquid and positioned to generate an income regardless of market conditions. Without green money, you may lack the income needed to meet your monthly expenses. In other words, green means go. This bucket can be made up of your banking, CDs, and fixed or fixed indexed annuities.

Red Money

Red money is the opposite of green money. It's earmarked for longer-term goals, with a higher risk tolerance for potential growth. These are the funds you shouldn't need within the next five to ten years, or longer. Red money is the money you can risk, the money you don't have to have to achieve your basic needs and can invest in goals like leaving your family a healthy inheritance, planning for the grandkids' college, or setting it aside for future use for health care or other expenses down the road. Red money is not usually ideal for income since it depends on the market environment.

These are more aggressive investments, like passive index funds or individual stocks. Without red money, you may not be able to grow your money enough to meet longer-term goals. If the market is down, you likely won't want to lock in your losses and sell off shares to provide income. In this case red means stop.

Yellow Money

For investments that fall in between green and red money, we unsurprisingly categorize them as yellow money. Yes, we know this analogy is cheesy, but we challenge you to find us a better one. Yellow money consists of investments that are generally more cautious, pay you more income to keep, and have less market volatility than red money investments. This could be a fixed-income strategy, an actively managed strategy, or even a basket of **blue-chip** dividend-paying stocks.

Like a yellow light at an intersection, we use caution with yellow money. It carries less risk than a pure growth account and can be used to generate a modest amount of income in most, if not all, market environments.

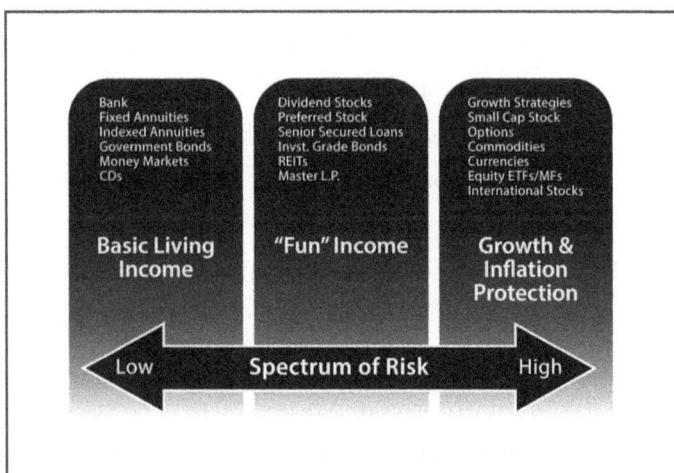

Bank Fixed Annuities Indexed Annuities Government Bonds Money Markets CDs	Dividend Stocks Preferred Stock Senior Secured Loans Invst. Grade Bonds REITs Master L.P.	Growth Strategies Small Cap Stock Options Commodities Currencies Equity ETFs/MFs International Stocks
Basic Living Income	**"Fun" Income**	**Growth & Inflation Protection**

Low ◀ **Spectrum of Risk** ▶ High

Once we have our green, red, and yellow money in mind, we consult the "spectrum of risk" chart above to explain these three different categories to our clients. As we stated, your green money is the money that is protected from the markets and is allocated for your everyday living expenses. As you shift to the right, the investments take on more risk, whether it be interest rate risk, credit risk, or market risk. The yellow money category is in the middle. Red money is the riskiest of the assets on the right side of the spectrum. When building a balanced plan, it's critical to understand how the different types of money work and balance each other out.

We break down money allocation because every client we work with is different. They all enter retirement with a different amount saved with different goals, risk tolerances, and time horizons. When we sit down with a client, the first thing we talk about is how we're going to generate income—and do it safely. Our clients are entering a new phase of their lives: the wealth distribution phase. Now they must put capital preservation and income generation before aggressive growth. We use the spectrum of risk chart to show that there is no one perfect investment, but using the right combination of these categories, we can build a retirement plan that accomplishes their retirement needs and goals.

By helping clients differentiate between "have to" money and "risk" money, we provide not just financial planning, but peace of mind, especially during market turbulence. It's a lot easier to stomach a market downturn when you know you don't need that money in the short term.

That's why we like to break down our clients' money into these categories to illustrate the different classifications of money—all on a single sheet of paper called the *Retirement Roadmap*. We developed the retirement roadmap to help our clients remember the purpose of their allocation and why we structured it that way.

At our firm we educate our clients so they know *how* their money works for them. We also assist them in assigning a purpose to each bucket of money. We feel that assigning a purpose to each bucket of money helps illustrate to our clients the differences between the multitude of investment vehicles, and the differences between green, yellow, and red money. Once our clients have developed a better sense of how their money works for them and their retirement goals, they sleep much better at night.

Flexibility is ingrained in our approach, allowing us to adapt to evolving client objectives or market conditions. Plans are fluid, ensuring alignment with our clients' ever-changing needs and circumstances.

If a client has a nice run of really good years with their red money and wants to pull some of those gains off the table and shift into less risky vehicles, we'll encourage them to do that if it fits with their plan. It depends on the situation, but in almost everyone's case, having some money protected from the swings of the market is essential.

No matter who you are or what your financial situation is, your financial advisor should be assisting you in building a portfolio that accomplishes your specific goals in retirement. This all begins with proper diversification and identifying which investment vehicles will work together to meet your needs. The trick is finding a retirement planner who can build a complex plan for your retirement needs that you can understand.

The KISS principle serves as our guiding light, reminding us to prioritize simplicity and clarity in all aspects of financial planning. By keeping things simple, we empower our clients to navigate the complexities of retirement with confidence and peace of mind.

Retirement Trivia

When categorizing money between red, yellow, and green, it is important to account for how each of the separate buckets of money is taxed. What term describes the strategy of strategically placing different types of investments in specific types of accounts to optimize tax efficiency?

    a. Asset Placement

    b. Portfolio Placement

    c. Asset Allocation

    d. Asset Location

The answer can be found on page 183.

Three Key Takeaways

1. Simplicity is important. People experience financial stress and anxiety because they don't understand their financial plans. Keeping financial planning simple and easy to understand is crucial, especially because people come from various backgrounds and may have different preferences for detail.

2. Categorizing your money. The concept of bucketing money into green money, red money, and yellow money helps clients understand the different roles their assets play in their financial plans. Green money represents essential living expenses; red money represents riskier, long-term goals; and yellow money represents cautious investments, a balanced approach to generate a modest income.

3. Flexibility and diversification. A well-designed retirement plan should be flexible, with the ability to adjust allocations when clients' goals or market conditions change. Diversification is essential to protect against underperformance in specific investments or sectors.

Questions for You

- Do you currently have a retirement plan? If so, how well do you understand your plan, and do you find it overly complex or difficult to grasp?
- Have you categorized your investments into green money, red money, and yellow money to clarify their roles and risks in your financial strategy? If not, is this a concept you would consider applying to your planning?
- Are you working with a financial advisor who not only provides reassurances but also educates you about the different investment vehicles and how they align with your specific retirement goals?

Notes:

NINE

How to Choose the Right Advisor

To accept good advice is but to increase one's own ability.

– Johann Wolfgang von Goethe

The transition from planning for retirement to actually retiring is a pivotal moment, and finding the right advisor can make all the difference. A good advisor not only possesses the necessary expertise but also operates with integrity, prioritizing the client's best interests above all else. Anyone can print a business card and call themselves a financial advisor, so finding a good financial advisor can take some work. If you don't know what questions to ask and what to expect from a good financial advisor, you can find yourself in a bad situation.

All too often in the financial world you think you're hiring someone with expertise, when you could be hiring someone who doesn't know the first thing about retirement planning—or worse, someone who does know what they're doing but is more interested in making money for themselves than for their clients. Fortunately, there are all sorts of knowledgeable, ethical financial advisors, but how do you find the right one? It takes time and research. If you don't know what questions to ask and what qualifications to look for, it could lead to you working with an advisor who isn't suited to satisfy your specific needs.

On the *Retirement Approved* podcast, we talk about how to plan for retirement, and we help listeners change their mindsets, as we do in this book, from growth to capital preservation and income. We like to focus on how much risk people should be taking in retirement versus how much income they should be producing from the same assets. We talk about Social Security, tax planning, inflation, and the various financial vehicles. People are invited to send in questions so we can jumpstart their retirement planning right on the air. We always get asked, "How do I go about finding a trusted advisor, and what questions should I be asking?"

This is a harder question than you may think. When looking for a new doctor or restaurant or any service, really, the typical person will google "Best doctor in Detroit" or "Best pizza in Detroit." You might find over 3,000 wonderful five-star reviews for Buddy's Pizza and be on your way to enjoying their historic deep dish.

It's not that simple when it comes to finding a financial advisor. Investment advisors haven't been allowed to provide or promote testimonials until recently. It makes sense. You wouldn't want to see fake five-star reviews when dealing with people's life savings. But this means it takes more effort than a simple internet search when searching for a trusted advisor.

The following list of questions are what you should be asking and what you should be looking for when you begin your search.

Is Your Financial Planner Operating under the Fiduciary or Suitability Standard?

A financial professional who works under the suitability standard is not required to work in your best interest. Suitability advisors use a handful of factors—such as an investor's age, risk tolerance, and net worth—to make recommendations they think are suitable, but they aren't required to work in the client's best interest when making recommendations. The "suitable" recommendation may perform in a way that meets your needs, but it may not be the best or lowest cost investment for you.

The suitability standard is a problem because the financial advisors working under that standard don't keep your best interests in mind, whereas planners operating under the fiduciary standard are required by law to do so. The suitability standard only requires a financial planner to know the client and recommend financial vehicles that are "suitable" to their clients rather than ideal.

The **fiduciary standard** requires the planner to put the client's best interest first, to practice diligence and good judgment, to provide full disclosure, to avoid conflict of interest, and to disclose and manage any conflicts of interest that might inevitably arise. They must do what is best for their client, period.

Think of it like buying an automobile. You go to the Kia dealership down the road and tell them you're looking for a four-wheel drive pickup truck. Kia doesn't make this vehicle, so the dealer suggests their SUV, sells it to you, and collects their commission. Under the suitability standard, they've sold you the car most suitable to you from their limited options. Under the fiduciary standard, the car dealer would be required to tell you to head over to Ford or GM, and they would find the exact truck that fits your needs, not find an SUV that is merely suitable.

What Level of Education Has the Financial Advisor Achieved?

As we previously mentioned, the bar for entry into the financial profession has been set quite low. It may be that the advisor passed a simple licensing exam to sell insurance or securities, which often doesn't require a college education or formal education. In contrast, some advisors put themselves through extensive educational programs to obtain designations such as **Certified Financial Planner™ (CFP®)**, **Chartered Financial Analyst (CFA)**, or **Chartered Financial Consultant (ChFC)**.

Just because you see a few letters after an advisor's name doesn't mean they've gone through a rigorous educational requirement like the designations mentioned above. The credentials that advisors hold may seem impressive on the surface, but when you dig a little deeper, you'll find that many awards and credentials can be bought or achieved through little coursework. For example, you could earn the following credentials in less than one month:

- CAC—Certified Annuity Consultant
- CSA—Certified Senior Advisor
- RFC—Registered Financial Consultant
- CWPP—Certified Wealth Preservation Planner
- APP—Asset Protection Planner
- CRFA—Certified Retirement Financial Advisor

The list goes on and on. Fortunately, **FINRA** has provided a list of each designation and the requirements to obtain them, which can be found at FINRA.org. (https://www.finra.org/investors/professional-designations).

Compared to the above designations that can be obtained fairly easily, the CFP® requires a bachelor's degree from an accredited college or university, as well as a two-year university level program through a CFP-registered program in the major personal financial planning areas, including:

- General principles of financial planning
- Insurance planning
- Investment planning
- Tax planning
- Retirement planning
- Estate planning
- Financial plan development requiring a presentation to the CFP® Board

This coursework takes about two years to complete. Once a financial planner has completed this coursework, they must pass the CFP® exam, a pass/fail seven-hour test. They then have to log six thousand hours of experience in the field or four thousand hours in an apprenticeship and complete thirty hours of continuing education every two years. Only then does a financial planner become a **Certified Financial Planner™** professional.

If you're considering working with a financial planner who is not a CFP® (or similar designation with rigorous standards), look at that list of classes again. Do you really want to work with someone who may or may not have training in retirement planning? A recent study by the CFP® Board found that 84 percent of consumers working with a CFP® professional are satisfied. That number drops to less than 50 percent for those working with an advisor who is not a CFP®. Asking an advisor about their education is fundamental in your search, and it should be the first question you ask.

How Much Experience Does Your Financial Planner Have?

Financial planner experience is a tricky one. You want a financial professional who's been around for a while, but maybe not too long. If you like a financial professional who's close to retirement age, make sure they have a succession plan and that you're acquainted with other planners at the firm.

According to a recent study by JD Power, a global leader in consumer insights, the average age of a financial advisor is fifty-five, and approximately one-fifth of advisors are sixty-five or older.[29] Think about it: If your advisor is fifty-five, and your retirement lasts thirty-plus years, you'll want to make sure they have a contingency plan. Better yet, you may want to establish a relationship with the younger advisors at the firm because one day they'll be your primary advisor.

A financial advisor understands how the market works and the impact of emotions like fear and greed on investing. Often, a financial advisor needs to adopt the role of psychologist, guiding clients away from impulsive buying and selling decisions. One of the primary duties of an advisor is to ensure commitment to the established plan and foster the continued compounding of assets. After all, years of diligent work have grown and compounded for years and years. Compound interest, often hailed as the "eighth wonder of the world," allows for exponential growth of your nest egg over your lifetime.

29   Edward Jones, "Technology, Social Media Critical to Bridging Financial Advisor Age Gap, J.D. Power Finds," J.D. Power, July 9, 2019, https://www.jdpower.com/business/press-releases/2019-us-financial-advisor-satisfaction-study.

Retirement Trivia

Our brains are not wired to comprehend exponential growth. Exponential growth is simply a snowball effect, where as time goes on, the growth rate keeps getting applied to a larger and larger amount, making the total grow faster and faster. A great way to illustrate this is to imagine folding a piece of paper in half. In reality, you can only fold a piece of paper in half seven times. But imagine for a second, if you could fold that piece of paper in half fifty times, what would the thickness of the paper be on the fiftieth fold?

    a.   the width of a 500-page book

    b.   the height of a six-foot human

    c.   the height of the Empire State Building

    d.   the distance from the earth to the sun

The answer can be found on page 185.

Is Your Financial Planner Independent or Attached to a Large Financial Services Firm?

Some financial professionals contract with and operate under the umbrella of a larger firm that creates and sells financial products and services. Others are employees of those firms. Independent financial advisors are not affiliated with any company, bank, or other corporate entity, so they aren't limited in the products they can offer.

No one provider has a lock on the best products in every category. You want someone who represents a multitude of companies and who can put together the best financial plan possible and fund it with all the latest and greatest vehicles.

Does Your Financial Planner Have Expertise in Retirement Planning?

If your financial planner is not an expert in retirement planning, why not seek out an advisor who has extensive experience or who works exclusively in retirement planning? Building toward retirement is one set of skills, while transitioning to retirement and protecting your money so that it lasts is another. Again, there are plenty of CFPs who focus on retirement planning or have plenty of experience in the field to pick from.

After you've found an advisor you think might be the right fit, common sense comes into play. You can tell a lot by meeting with a potential advisor and seeing what their process is and how your philosophies align. If they're more interested in selling you financial products than helping you plan and budget for your retirement, that will become apparent quickly enough. If they aren't terribly concerned with you as a person and your goals for retirement, that will also become clear. If their process is complicated or unclear, that might also be a bad sign. If you don't get a clear answer when asked how they are compensated, that is also a bad sign. Typical compensation structures are **fee only, fee based,** and **commission only**.

Although retirement planning can be quite complex, the process doesn't have to be. We try to make our process as simple and straightforward as possible.

Every advisor has their own process. In a first meeting with us, we get to know the client, their goals for retirement, and their overall financial health. In the second meeting we review their current investment allocation and discuss the associated fees and underlying risks. We tend to find that the client may be carrying more risk than they're comfortable with or are paying more than they thought. We'll discuss other concerns such as income goals, Social Security, loss of income, long-term care, and wealth transfer. From this point, if the clients want to move forward with our firm, we have multiple investment meetings, moving slowly through the design of the investment/retirement plan. We do this to ensure that our clients not only understand how the plan works but also feel comfortable with it.

Throughout this process we talk in detail about the different investment vehicles we're using so our clients don't leave our office confused or wondering what's actually happening with their money. We want them to be able to go home and explain every aspect of their plan to their family, not simply say they found retirement planners they trust with their money.

As part of the pre-planning process before clients come in for their first meeting, we send out materials explaining what they can expect when they come in. One of those items, the Retirement Roadmap Review, details how we operate and what the planning process entails. It shows our process from our introductory call all the way to the last planning meeting, so our clients know exactly to expect when engaging our services.

The last and perhaps most important step is to research the potential financial advisors themselves. The Security and Exchange Commission's Investment Adviser Public Disclosure website (https://adviserinfo.sec.gov/) and the FINRA BrokerCheck (https://brokercheck.finra.org/) website provide excellent background checks on potential financial advisors. If an advisor you're considering has ever been sued by a client or has been the subject of a lawsuit, that will come up. If they've ever gone bankrupt or have broken the law, you can find that too. If they've ever been involved in a scam or had a client bring a lawsuit over an unsuitable investment, guess what? That will pop up as well.

If you don't use these tools to investigate potential advisors, regardless of the boxes they might check, you could be working with someone you shouldn't trust.

Finding the right financial advisor can be a stressful experience. Ask the right questions, use common sense, do a little research on your own, and you'll find the right advisor for you. What's right for you, of course, depends on the person, but the best financial advisors follow a detailed process and get to know their clients and their goals. They should always put the best interests of their clients first and take pleasure from helping their clients get the most out of their retirement.

Three Key Takeaways

1. Choose the right financial advisor. The process of transitioning from retirement planning to retirement itself involves finding a trustworthy and knowledgeable financial advisor. Find a quality advisor, because they play a significant role in securing your financial future.

2. Understand standard of care. It's important to understand the difference between advisors operating under the fiduciary standard and those under the suitability standard. Advisors held to the fiduciary standard are legally obligated to act in the best interests of their clients, while those under the suitability standard may not be required to do so.

3. Inquire about your advisor's educational background and experience. Some credentials and designations in the financial industry may have lower educational requirements, while others, like the **Certified Financial Planner™ (CFP®)**, involve rigorous coursework and testing.

Questions for You

- What is the standard of care your financial advisor operates under: fiduciary or suitability? How does this affect their recommendations and decisions regarding your financial planning?
- What is the educational background and experience of your financial advisor?
- Does your financial advisor hold any industry-recognized designations?
- Does your financial advisor have a level of education and experience that aligns with your retirement planning needs and goals?
- What is your financial advisor's expertise in retirement planning?
- Does your financial advisor focus exclusively on retirement?

Notes:

(TEN)
Conclusion—Your Retirement Awaits

Retirement may be an ending, a closing,
but it is also a new beginning.

– Catherine Pulsifer

As we reach the final pages of *Retirement Approved*, it is our sincere hope that this journey through the intricacies of financial planning for retirement has left you empowered and equipped with the knowledge to craft a secure and fulfilling future. The concept of "retirement approved" extends beyond a mere stamp of financial adequacy; it encompasses the holistic and strategic approach we've explored together.

In these chapters, we discussed a myriad of elements that shape a successful retirement plan—from understanding investment strategies and navigating potential pitfalls, to demystifying the process of selecting a trusted advisor. Each topic has been a building block, contributing to the overarching theme of achieving a retirement that is financially secure and personally satisfying.

The essence of being retirement approved is more than the numbers in your financial plan. It's about the quality of life you lead during your golden years. It's about making choices that align with your values, aspirations, and dreams. It's about creating a plan that adapts to life's twists and turns, allowing you the flexibility to savor the fruits of your labor.

As you embark on this significant phase of life, remember that approval comes not only from financial acumen but from a well-rounded approach. Embrace the joy of balancing financial responsibility with the pursuit of your passions, whether it be travel, hobbies, or spending quality time with loved ones.

The retirement approved stamp may signify the final chapter of this book, but it's also the beginning of a new chapter in your life. It's a testament to your commitment to thoughtful planning, resilience in the face of challenges, and the wisdom to seek the guidance needed for success.

May your retirement be a canvas onto which you paint the masterpiece of your desires, free from the worry of financial uncertainty. Congratulations on taking the steps to ensure that your retirement is retirement approved. With your newfound knowledge and a well-crafted plan, your retirement is destined to be extraordinary. May this next chapter be the most rewarding one yet!

Subscribe to the *Retirement Approved* Podcast

Discover the roadmap to financial freedom with *Retirement Approved*, a podcast curated for your retirement planning journey. Led by the expertise of Steven Paul, CFP® and Matt Paul, CFP®, this podcast is your compass through the intricacies of securing a comfortable retirement. From insightful investment strategies to navigating tax complexities and making thoughtful lifestyle choices, Steven and Matt bring decades of experience to the table, ensuring that every episode equips you with practical knowledge.

Explore a vast spectrum of topics in the realm of retirement planning—demystifying the financial landscape and empowering you to make informed decisions. With a dynamic and approachable style, Steven and Matt break down complex financial concepts, making them accessible to everyone, regardless of their financial background. This podcast is not just a source of information; it's your companion on the journey to financial independence.

Subscribe to *Retirement Approved* on your favorite podcast platform to stay updated with the latest episodes. Join our community of like-minded individuals, connect with us on social media, and be part of the ongoing conversation. Your questions and feedback are not just welcome; they are an integral part of our mission to guide you towards a secure and fulfilling retirement.

The full episode archive can be found at:
RetirementApproved.com

Retirement Trivia Answers

Chapter 1

When was the concept of retirement created?

Answer: C) The late 1800s

According to SSA.gov:

Germany became the first nation in the world to adopt an old-age social insurance program in 1889, designed by Germany's Chancellor, Otto von Bismarck. The idea was first put forward, at Bismarck's behest, in 1881 by Germany's Emperor, William the First, in a groundbreaking letter to the German Parliament. William wrote: ". . . those who are disabled from work by age and invalidity have a well-grounded claim to care from the state."

One persistent myth about the German program is that it adopted age sixty-five as the standard retirement age because that was Bismarck's age. In fact, Germany initially set age seventy as the retirement age (and Bismarck himself was seventy-four at the time) and it was not until twenty-seven years later (in 1916) that the age was lowered to sixty-five. By that time, Bismarck had been dead for eighteen years.[30]

For a retiree with $1 million, the 4 percent rule states that a retiree could reasonably expect to take $40,000 out of the portfolio on an annual basis. During a low interest rate environment, what would be considered a safe withdrawal rate?

Answer: B) 2.4 percent

In a 2020 interview with ThinkAdvisor, Wade Pfau, PhD, CFA, states that because of high market valuations, interest rate lows, and various other factors, the 4 percent rule of thumb for income withdrawal in retirement has shriveled to only 2.4 percent for investors taking a moderate amount of risk.[31]

Chapter 2

Eighty percent of retirees in better health report having a positive experience in retirement, compared to only ___ percent of those who are in poorer health.

Answer is C) 59 percent

A 2015 study by MassMutual concluded that 80 percent of retirees in better health report having a positive experience in retirement, compared to only 59 percent

---

30 "Age 65 Retirement," Frequently Asked Questions, Social Security Administration, https://www.ssa.gov/history/age65.html.

31 Jane Wollman Rusoff, "Wade Pfau: Pandemic Tears Up 4% Rule," ThinkAdvisor, April 14, 2020, https://www.thinkadvisor.com/2020/04/14/wade-pfau-virus-crisis-has-slashed-4-rule-nearly-in-half/.

of those who are in poorer health.[32] The study also concluded that 87 percent of retirees in better health felt secure at retirement versus 69 percent of those in poorer health.

Chapter 3

If your portfolio loses 40 percent of its value, you'll need to make a gain of more than ____percent to get back to even.

Answer: C) 66.67 percent

Solution:

If your portfolio loses 40 percent, it means you have 60 percent of its original value left.

To get back to even, you need to figure out how much the remaining 60 percent needs to grow.

Divide 100 percent (the original value) by 60 percent (the remaining value) to find out how many times the remaining amount needs to grow to get back to 100 percent.

Subtract 1 from the result to find out the actual growth needed as a fraction.

Multiply the result by 100 to get the percentage growth needed to break even.

---

32 https://www.massmutual.com/global/media/shared/doc/health-wealth-happi-ness-report-2015.pdf

Chapter 4

On January 31, 1940, the first monthly retirement check was issued to Ida May Fuller of Ludlow, Vermont. Ida paid a total of $24.75 into the Social Security program.

How much was paid out to her in Social Security benefits?

Answer: D) $22,228

According to SSA.gov: "Miss Fuller, a Legal Secretary, retired in November 1939. She started collecting benefits in January 1940 at age 65 and lived to be 100 years old, dying in 1975.

Ida May Fuller worked for three years under the Social Security program. The accumulated taxes on her salary during those three years was a total of $24.75. Her initial monthly check was $22.54. During her lifetime she collected a total of $22,888.92 in Social Security benefits."[33]

What term describes the phenomenon where manufacturers reduce the size or quantity of a product while keeping its price the same?

Answer: B) Shrinkflation

Shrinkflation is a sneaky tactic used by manufacturers and retailers to maintain the price of a product while reducing its size or quantity. Essentially, it's a form of

---

33 "Research Note #3: Details of Ida May Fuller's Payroll Tax Contributions," Agency History, Social Security Administration, prepared July 1996, https://www.ssa.gov/history/idapayroll.html.

inflation where consumers end up paying the same amount (or sometimes more) for less product.

Here are a few funny (but realistic) examples of shrinkflation:

"Air-filled" potato chip bags: You open up a bag of potato chips only to find that it's mostly air! While the bag looks the same size as before, the actual quantity of chips inside has decreased.

"Fun-sized" candy bars: Have you noticed how those candy bars seem to get smaller and smaller every year? It's not just your imagination—it's shrinkflation at work!

"Trimmed" tube of toothpaste: You squeeze your toothpaste tube and realize that it's not lasting as long as it used to. That's because the manufacturer has decreased the amount of toothpaste in the tube while charging the same price.

"Slimmed-down" cereal boxes: You reach for your favorite breakfast cereal, but you notice that the box feels lighter than usual. Sure enough, when you check the label, you realize that the manufacturer has reduced the amount of cereal inside while keeping the price the same.

Chapter 5

What common behavioral bias, often leading to investor underperformance, describes the tendency of individuals to hold on to losing investments for too long and sell winning investments too quickly?

Answer: A) The Disposition Effect

The disposition effect refers to the tendency of investors to hold on to losing investments for too long and sell winning investments too quickly. This behavior stems from a reluctance to realize losses, which can lead to a portfolio comprised of underperforming assets.

Loss aversion is a related phenomenon where individuals feel the pain of losses more acutely than the pleasure of gains, causing them to prioritize avoiding losses. Anchoring is a cognitive bias where individuals rely too heavily on the first piece of information they receive when making decisions, often leading to suboptimal outcomes in investment choices. The gambler's fallacy is the mistaken belief that future outcomes are influenced by past events, such as expecting a streak of losses to be followed by a streak of wins. In investing, this fallacy can lead to poor decision-making, as past performance does not guarantee future results. These cognitive biases and fallacies can contribute to investor underperformance and hinder effective decision-making in financial markets.

Chapter 6

Placing an annuity in an after-tax account offers the significant advantage of deferring taxes on gains until withdrawal. However, what potential drawbacks might arise from this arrangement?

Answer: B) Gains are taxed as ordinary income.

One potential drawback of placing an annuity in an after-tax account is that gains are taxed as ordinary income upon withdrawal. This means that any growth in the annuity is taxed at the individual's ordinary income tax rate at the time of withdrawal. It is also important to note that upon death, beneficiaries do not receive a step up in basis, and will also be taxed as ordinary income.

Now, let's explore why the wrong answers are incorrect:

A. "Gains are taxed as qualified dividends when withdrawing." This answer is incorrect because annuity gains are not typically taxed as qualified dividends. Qualified dividends are taxed at lower capital gains tax rates, but reserved for equities of US corporation or a qualified foreign corporation and meet specific holding period requirements.

C. "Gains are withdrawn last." This answer is incorrect because it refers to the method of withdrawing funds from an account, specifically using the first in, first out (FIFO) method. Annuities are taxed as last in, first out

(LIFO) method, meaning gains distributions will be the first withdrawals out of the annuity contract.

D. "Gains are tax-free after RMD age." This answer is incorrect because annuity gains are not tax-free after the required minimum distribution (RMD) age. Gains are taxed as ordinary income upon withdrawal, regardless of the individual's age.

Chapter 7

When assessing portfolio volatility, standard deviation provides a confidence interval indicating that returns will typically fall within a certain range about 95 percent of the time. Consequently, approximately 5 percent of the time, returns may deviate beyond this range—specifically, 2.5 percent of the time, returns might be worse than anticipated, while 2.5 percent of the time, returns could exceed expectations. What term is commonly used to describe this phenomenon?

Answer: D) Tail Risk

Tail risk refers to the risk of extreme or unexpected events occurring that have a significant impact on investment returns. These events, often referred to as "fat tail" events, lie on the extreme ends, or tails, of the probability distribution curve of potential outcomes. Tail risk events are typically rare but can have severe consequences, leading to substantial losses for investors. Examples of tail risk events include market crashes, financial crises, geopolitical conflicts, natural disasters, and other unforeseen events that can cause widespread disruptions to financial markets and economies.

Chapter 8

When categorizing money between red, yellow, and green, it is important to account for how each of the separate buckets of money is taxed. What term describes the strategy of strategically placing different types of investments in specific types of accounts to optimize tax efficiency?

Answer: D) Asset Location

Let's review some pros and cons of various assets in IRA/NQ accounts:

Placing bonds in tax-advantaged accounts like IRAs makes sense as interest income generated by bonds is taxed at ordinary income rates. Keeping high-income assets sheltered in tax-advantaged accounts helps minimize the tax impact. Stocks, on the other hand, are often better suited for non-qualified (NQ) accounts. Qualified dividends and long-term capital gains from stocks enjoy more favorable tax rates than ordinary income. Placing them in NQ accounts takes advantage of these preferential tax rates.

In non-qualified (NQ) accounts, annuities offer tax-deferred growth, allowing earnings to accumulate without immediate taxation. Annuities in NQ accounts can result in gains being taxed as ordinary income upon distribution. This may lead to a higher tax liability compared to capital gains tax rates. In NQ accounts, annuity gains are not eligible for a step-up in basis upon inheritance. Beneficiaries may inherit the annuity with its original cost basis, potentially leading to higher capital gains taxes if they choose to sell. Non-qualified Stretch annuities are financial products designed to allow beneficiaries to receive distributions over their lifetime, potentially stretching out the tax-deferral benefits of the original account.

Conversely, annuities within IRAs can be strategically used for income planning. Phasing out IRA accounts in retirement allows for a steady income stream, potentially in the early years when other income sources may be lower. Not to mention, we have been in historically lower than average tax environments, so there is a strong likelihood tax rates will increase in the future.

Roth IRAs are a great place for high-growth assets due to their tax-free nature. By allocating assets with significant growth potential to Roth IRAs, individuals aim to maximize the tax-free benefits, especially for wealth transfer purposes. This strategic allocation ensures that beneficiaries receive the assets tax-free, offering a powerful tool for passing wealth to the next generation. Hypothetically speaking, if your income for the year is maxing out your current bracket, Roth IRAs allow you the flexibility to generate income without going into higher tax brackets. As it stands now, when the account owner passes away, in most cases a non-spouse beneficiary has the option to defer and grow the account over the ten-year distribution period without forced RMDs. The only requirement is that the Roth IRA be distributed by December 31 of the tenth year.

Chapter 9

Our brains are not wired to comprehend exponential growth. Exponential growth is simply a snowball effect, where as time goes on, the growth rate keeps getting applied to a larger and larger amount, making the total grow faster and faster. A great way to illustrate this is to imagine folding a piece of paper in half. In reality, you can only fold a piece of paper in half seven times. But imagine for a second, if you could fold that piece of paper in half fifty times, what would the thickness of the paper be on the fiftieth fold?

Answer: D) the distance from the earth to the sun

Let's break down the math:

When you fold a piece of paper in half, its thickness doubles. Let's assume the thickness of a standard piece of paper is about 0.1 millimeters (mm). After the first fold, the thickness is 0.1 mm ... 0.2 mm. After the second fold, it's 0.2 mm ... 0.4 mm. And so on.

After fifty folds, the thickness would be 0.1 mm * 2^50, which is roughly 1.13 x 10^13 millimeters, or about 113 million kilometers. Now, the average distance from the Earth to the Sun (also known as an astronomical unit or AU) is about 149.6 million kilometers. So, by the fiftieth fold, the thickness of the paper would actually exceed the distance from the Earth to the Sun!

This exponential growth is similar to compounding interest, where your money grows exponentially over time. Just as each fold doubles the thickness of the paper, compounding interest adds interest to the principal, leading to exponential growth of your investment over time.

Glossary

4 Percent Withdrawal Rate: Also known as the 4 percent rule or the Safe Withdrawal Rate (SWR), is a guideline used in retirement planning to determine a sustainable annual withdrawal rate from a retirement portfolio. The rule was popularized by financial planner William Bengen in the early 1990s. The basic premise of the 4 percent rule is that retirees can withdraw 4 percent of their initial retirement portfolio balance in the first year of retirement, adjusting this amount annually for inflation thereafter, without running out of money over a thirty-year retirement period.

401(k): A 401(k) is an employer-sponsored retirement savings plan that allows employees to contribute a portion of their pre-tax income to the plan, often with the option for employers to match a portion of the contributions. Contributions to a traditional 401(k) reduce taxable income in the year they are made, and investments within the account grow tax-deferred until withdrawals are made in retirement, at which point they are taxed as ordinary income. Some employers also offer

Roth 401(k) options, which allow employees to make after-tax contributions and potentially receive tax-free withdrawals in retirement, similar to a Roth IRA. 401(k) plans typically offer a selection of investment options chosen by the employer, such as mutual funds, index funds, and target-date funds.

Active Management: An investment strategy in which a portfolio manager or investment team makes specific decisions to buy or sell securities within a portfolio in an attempt to outperform a benchmark or achieve superior returns compared to the broader market. In active management, portfolio managers rely on their expertise, research, analysis, and market insights to identify undervalued or overvalued securities, anticipate market trends, and capitalize on investment opportunities. Active managers may engage in various strategies, including stock picking, sector rotation, market timing, and tactical asset allocation, to generate alpha, or excess returns, relative to a benchmark index or peer group. Active management contrasts with passive management, where investment portfolios are designed to replicate the performance of a benchmark index rather than attempting to outperform it. While active management offers the potential for higher returns, it also entails higher costs, including management fees and trading expenses, and presents the risk of underperformance compared to passive alternatives.

Artificial Intelligence (AI): AI refers to the simulation of human intelligence processes by machines, especially computer systems. These processes include learning (the acquisition of information and rules for using the information), reasoning (using rules to reach approximate or definite conclusions), and self-correction. AI encompasses a wide range of technologies and applications, including machine learning, natural language processing, computer vision, robotics, expert systems, and more. Machine learning, a subset of AI, involves the development of algorithms that enable computers to learn from and make predictions or decisions based on data, without being explicitly programmed.

Annual Percentage Rate (APR): A standardized measure that represents the annualized cost of borrowing. APR includes not only the interest rate charged on a loan or credit card, but also any additional fees or charges associated with the loan, such as origination fees or closing costs. It provides borrowers with a comprehensive measure of the true cost of borrowing over the course of a year, allowing them to compare different loan offers more effectively. a high APR can be detrimental to borrowers by increasing borrowing costs, imposing financial strain, reducing affordability, increasing the risk of default, and negatively impacting creditworthiness. It's important for borrowers to carefully consider the APR when comparing loan offers and to borrow responsibly within their means.

Assets Under Management (AUM): AUM refers to the total market value of assets that an investment firm manages on behalf of its clients. These assets typically include various types of investments such as stocks, bonds, ETFs, mutual funds, and other financial instruments.

Backdoor Roth IRA: A backdoor Roth IRA is a strategy used by high-income individuals to contribute to a Roth IRA indirectly, bypassing the income limits that would otherwise prevent direct contributions. The process involves making nondeductible contributions to a traditional IRA and then converting those funds into a Roth IRA. Since there are no income limits on Roth IRA conversions, individuals can utilize this strategy to take advantage of the tax-free growth and withdrawals offered by Roth IRAs.

Bipartisan Budget Act of 2015: The Bipartisan Budget Act of 2015 is a federal law passed by Congress and signed into law by President Barack Obama in November 2015. It made various changes to federal spending, revenue, and budget policies, including adjustments to Social Security Disability Insurance (SSDI) funding, Medicare premiums, and certain retirement benefit provisions.

Blue-chip Stocks: Blue-chips stocks are shares of large, well-established, financially stable companies with a history of consistent earnings, dividends, and a strong market presence. These companies are typically leaders in their respective industries and are considered to be relatively low-risk investments compared to smaller, less-established companies. Blue-chip stocks often have a track record of stable performance and are known for their ability to weather economic downturns. Investors often seek out blue-chip stocks for their potential for long-term capital appreciation and income generation through dividends. Examples of blue-chip stocks include companies like Coca-Cola, Apple, Johnson & Johnson, and Microsoft.

Bonds: Bonds are debt securities issued by governments, municipalities, or corporations to raise capital. When you buy a bond, you're essentially lending money to the issuer for a predetermined period, during which the issuer pays you interest at regular intervals (coupon payments). At the bond's maturity, the issuer repays the principal amount. Bonds are generally considered lower-risk investments compared to stocks because they offer fixed interest payments and repayment of principal, but they still carry risks such as interest rate risk and credit risk.

Bucketing: Also known as the bucket strategy or bucketing method, is a retirement planning strategy that involves dividing a retiree's investment portfolio into multiple "buckets" or compartments, each earmarked for specific purposes or time horizons. Each bucket is allocated different types of investments and strategies tailored to meet different financial goals and needs during retirement.

Buy and Hold: An investment strategy in which an investor purchases securities, such as stocks, bonds, or mutual funds, and holds onto them for an extended period of time, typically years or even decades, regardless of short-term market fluctuations. With the buy and hold strategy, investors aim to capitalize on the long-term growth potential of their investments and are less concerned with short-term price movements or market timing. Instead of actively trading or trying to time the market, buy and hold investors focus on selecting high-quality investments with strong fundamentals and holding onto them through market ups and downs. This strategy is often associated with a passive investing approach and is based on the belief that over the long term, financial markets tend to rise and that staying invested for the long haul can lead to favorable investment returns. Buy and hold is commonly used in retirement planning and wealth accumulation strategies, as it allows investors to benefit from the power of compounding and the growth potential of the broader economy over time.

CDs (Certificates of Deposit): CDs are time deposits offered by banks and credit unions. When you purchase a CD, you agree to deposit a certain amount of money for a specific period, known as the term or maturity period, which can range from a few months to several years. In return, the financial institution pays you interest at a fixed rate, typically higher than regular savings accounts. CDs are considered low-risk investments because they are insured by the Federal Deposit Insurance Corporation (FDIC) in the United States up to a certain limit, making them a popular choice for conservative investors seeking steady returns. However, withdrawing funds from a CD before its maturity may result in penalties.

CFA (Chartered Financial Analyst): The Chartered Financial Analyst (CFA) designation is a globally recognized professional credential awarded by the CFA Institute to investment professionals who have completed a rigorous program of study and examination. CFAs are trained in advanced investment analysis, portfolio management, and financial decision-making. The CFA program covers a wide range of topics, including ethics, quantitative methods, economics, financial reporting and analysis, corporate finance, equity and fixed income analysis, derivatives, alternative investments, and portfolio management. CFAs are commonly employed in roles such as portfolio managers, research analysts, investment advisors, and risk managers.

CFP (Certified Financial Planner): A Certified Financial Planner (CFP) is a professional designation awarded by the Certified Financial Planner Board of Standards, Inc. (CFP Board) to individuals who meet education, examination, experience, and ethics requirements. CFPs are trained to provide comprehensive financial planning services to individuals and families, including retirement planning, investment management, tax planning, estate planning, and insurance planning. CFPs adhere to a fiduciary standard, meaning they are required to act in their clients' best interests at all times.

Charitable Remainder Trusts (CRTs): A charitable remainder trust is a type of irrevocable trust that allows individuals to transfer assets, such as cash, securities, or real estate, to the trust while retaining an income stream for themselves or other beneficiaries for a specified period (typically their lifetime or a term of years). After the termination of the trust, the remaining assets are distributed to one or more designated charitable beneficiaries. CRTs offer benefits such as potential tax savings, the ability to generate income for beneficiaries, and the opportunity to support charitable causes.

ChFC (Chartered Financial Consultant): The Chartered Financial Consultant (ChFC) designation is a professional credential awarded by the American College of Financial Services to individuals who complete a series of courses and examinations covering various aspects of financial planning, including insurance, retirement planning, estate planning, taxation, and investments. ChFCs are trained to provide comprehensive financial planning services to individuals, families, and businesses, focusing on holistic financial solutions tailored to clients' needs and goals.

Chronic Care Rider: A chronic care rider is an optional provision available with some life insurance policies that provides additional benefits to policyholders who experience chronic illnesses or conditions that require long-term care. This rider typically allows policyholders to access a portion of the death benefit to cover qualifying long-term care expenses, such as nursing home care, assisted living, or home health care services.

Churning: Churning is a deceptive practice used by some unethical financial advisors or brokers to generate excessive trading activity in a client's account for the purpose of generating commissions or fees. Churning involves buying and selling securities frequently, often without regard for the client's investment objectives or best interests. It can result in unnecessary transaction costs, tax consequences, and erosion of the client's investment returns.

Commission-Only Advisor: Commission-only financial advisors are compensated exclusively through commissions or sales charges earned from the sale of financial products to clients. These advisors do not charge clients directly for advisory services but instead receive compensation when clients purchase specific financial products, such as mutual funds, annuities, insurance policies, or other investments. Commission-only advisors may have incentives to recommend products that generate higher commissions, which can create conflicts of interest and potentially result in recommendations that are not in the best interests of the client.

Consumer Price Index (CPI): The CPI is a measure of the average change over time in the prices paid by urban consumers for a basket of goods and services. The CPI is widely used as an indicator of inflation, which is the rate at which the general level of prices for goods and services is rising. The CPI is calculated by the Bureau of Labor Statistics (BLS) in the United States based on data collected from thousands of retail establishments and service providers across the country. The basket of goods and services included in the CPI represents the spending patterns of urban consumers and is divided into various categories, such as food, housing, transportation, and health care. Changes in the CPI are closely monitored by economists, policymakers, businesses, and investors as a key measure of inflationary pressures in the economy. Increases in the CPI indicate rising prices and potential inflationary trends, while decreases suggest falling prices and deflationary pressures. The Federal Reserve and other central banks use CPI data to inform monetary policy decisions, such as setting interest rates, to help maintain price stability and support economic growth.

Correlation: In investing, correlation measures the degree to which the price movements of two different assets or investments are related or move in tandem with each other. Correlation is expressed as a numerical value ranging from -1 to +1. A correlation of +1 indicates a perfect positive correlation, meaning that the two assets move in perfect synchronization, while a correlation of -1 indicates a perfect negative correlation, meaning that the two assets move in opposite directions. A correlation of 0 suggests no relationship between the movements of the two assets.

Covered Call: A covered call is an options trading strategy where an investor owns the underlying asset (such as stocks) and sells call options against it. By selling call options, the investor receives a premium from the buyer, who gains the right to purchase the underlying asset at a predetermined price (strike price) within a specified period (until expiration). The investor, in turn, is obligated to sell the asset if the option buyer chooses to exercise their right. Covered calls are often used by investors to generate income from their existing stock holdings while potentially limiting the upside potential if the stock price rises above the strike price.

Cryptocurrency: Crypto is a type of digital or virtual currency that uses cryptography for security and operates on decentralized networks based on blockchain technology. Unlike traditional currencies issued by governments (fiat currencies), cryptocurrencies are typically not controlled by any central authority, such as a central bank. Instead, they rely on distributed ledger technology, where transactions are recorded on a public ledger across a network of computers. Cryptocurrencies leverage cryptographic techniques to secure transactions, control the creation of new units, and verify the transfer of assets. They offer various features, including decentralization, transparency, immutability, and potentially lower transaction costs compared to traditional financial systems.

Do-It-Yourselfer: A do-it-yourselfer, or DIYer, is an individual who takes a hands-on approach to managing their own financial affairs, including investments, retirement planning, budgeting, and other aspects of personal finance, without relying on professional financial advisors or wealth managers for guidance or assistance. DIY investors typically research investment options, make their own investment decisions, and execute trades without the involvement of a financial advisor or broker. They may utilize online resources, financial publications, investment forums, and software tools to educate themselves and analyze investment opportunities. While DIY investing can offer cost savings and greater control over investment decisions, it also requires a significant time commitment, financial literacy, and the ability to handle the complexities and risks of managing one's own finances.

Donor Advised Funds (DAFs): A donor-advised fund is a charitable giving vehicle administered by a public charity or financial institution. Individuals can contribute cash, securities, or other assets to the fund and receive an immediate tax deduction for the value of the donated assets. The donor can then recommend grants to qualified charities over time, allowing for flexibility in charitable giving. DAFs offer benefits such as potential tax savings, simplicity of administration, and the ability to invest the assets for potential growth, enhancing the impact of charitable contributions.

Duration: Bond duration is a measure of a bond's sensitivity to changes in interest rates. It represents the weighted average time it takes for a bond's cash flows (interest payments and principal repayment) to be received, taking into account the present value of those cash flows and their timing. Bond duration helps investors assess the interest rate risk associated with a bond investment; bonds with longer durations are more sensitive to changes in interest rates, while bonds with shorter durations are less sensitive.

Employee Retirement Income Security Act (ERISA): ERISA is a federal law enacted in 1974 that sets standards for the protection of individuals' rights and interests in employer-sponsored retirement plans, such as 401(k) plans and pension plans. It establishes guidelines for plan administration, reporting, disclosure, and fiduciary responsibilities to ensure that employees receive promised benefits and that retirement plan assets are managed prudently.

Exchange-Traded funds (ETFs): An exchange-traded fund (ETF) is a type of investment fund that is traded on stock exchanges, much like individual stocks. ETFs typically hold assets such as stocks, bonds, commodities, or a combination of these, and they often aim to replicate the performance of a specific index, sector, or asset class. ETFs provide investors with diversification, flexibility, and liquidity, as they can be bought and sold throughout the trading day at market prices (unlike mutual funds).

Fear of Missing Out (FOMO): This term refers to the anxiety or apprehension that individuals feel when they believe others are experiencing something desirable, and they fear being left out of the opportunity. In the context of investing, FOMO can lead investors to make impulsive decisions, such as buying into a rapidly rising stock or asset, out of fear that they will miss out on potential gains. This fear can sometimes override rational decision-making and lead to poor investment choices.

Federal Reserve: The Federal Reserve, often referred to as the Fed, is the central banking system of the United States. It is responsible for conducting monetary policy to promote stable prices, maximum employment, and moderate long-term interest rates. The Federal Reserve also supervises and regulates banks and other financial institutions to ensure the safety and soundness of the banking system.

Fee-Based Advisor: Fee-based financial advisors receive compensation from both the fees they charge their clients for advisory services and commissions or other forms of compensation from the sale of financial products. While fee-based advisors may provide fee-based advisory services, they also have the option to earn additional income by selling products such as mutual funds, annuities, insurance policies, or other investment products. This dual compensation structure can create potential conflicts of interest, but also allows the advisor to expand product offerings to commissionable products which may serve the client's best interest.

Fee-Only Advisor: Fee-only financial advisors are compensated solely by the fees they charge their clients for the services they provide. These fees may be based on a percentage of assets under management (AUM), an hourly rate, or a flat fee for specific services. Fee-only advisors do not receive any commissions or other forms of compensation from financial product providers, such as mutual fund companies or insurance companies.

Fiduciary Standard: The fiduciary standard is a legal and ethical obligation that requires financial advisors to act in their clients' best interests at all times and to put their clients' interests ahead of their own. Fiduciary advisors are held to a higher standard of care and must provide advice and recommendations that are in the best interests of their clients, free from conflicts of interest. Fiduciary duty encompasses principles of honesty, integrity, loyalty, and diligence, and applies to both registered investment advisors (RIAs) and certain financial professionals providing investment advice, such as CFPs. The fiduciary standard is contrasted with the suitability standard, which requires financial professionals to recommend products that are suitable for clients' needs and objectives, but does not necessarily require recommendations to be in the client's best interests.

FINRA (Financial Industry Regulatory Authority): FINRA is a self-regulatory organization (SRO) that oversees and regulates brokerage firms and individual brokers in the United States. It was formed in 2007 through the consolidation of the National Association of Securities Dealers (NASD) and the regulatory functions of the New York Stock Exchange (NYSE). FINRA's mission is to protect investors and ensure the integrity of the securities industry by enforcing rules and regulations, licensing brokers and brokerage firms, conducting examinations and investigations, and providing education and resources to investors.

Fixed Annuity or Multi-Year Guaranteed Annuity (MYGA): A type of annuity contract offered by insurance companies that guarantees a fixed interest rate for a specific period, typically ranging from two to ten years. With a MYGA, the insurance company guarantees the principal amount invested, as well as the interest rate, for the duration of the contract. MYGAs provide a predictable rate of return and can be used as a conservative investment option for individuals seeking stable, guaranteed income over a defined period.

Fixed Indexed Annuities: A fixed indexed annuity (FIA) is a type of annuity contract that offers investors the potential for growth linked to the performance of a specific stock market index, such as the S&P 500, while also providing downside protection against market losses. With an FIA, the annuity issuer credits interest to the contract based on the performance of the underlying index, subject to certain limitations, such as caps, participation rates, or spreads. Unlike variable annuities, where the investment returns are directly tied to the performance of underlying investment options, FIAs offer a level of protection by guaranteeing a minimum interest rate or floor, ensuring that the annuity holder will not lose principal due to market downturns. FIAs are often used as retirement income vehicles, providing investors with the potential for market-linked returns along with downside protection and guaranteed income payments in retirement.

Full Retirement Age (FRA): Full retirement age refers to the age at which individuals become eligible to receive full Social Security retirement benefits. It varies depending on the year of birth and is gradually increasing under current law. For example, for individuals born in 1960 or later, the FRA is sixty-seven.

Health Savings Account (HSA): A health savings account is a tax-advantaged savings account available to individuals with high-deductible health insurance plans. HSAs are designed to help individuals save for qualified medical expenses, both current and future, such as deductibles, copayments, and certain other medical costs. Contributions to an HSA are tax-deductible, earnings on investments within the account grow tax-free, and withdrawals used for qualified medical expenses are tax-free as well. HSAs offer flexibility, as funds can be rolled over from year to year and can be invested to potentially grow over time.

Hedge Fund: A hedge fund is an investment fund typically open to a limited range of investors and employs a variety of strategies to generate returns. Unlike mutual funds, hedge funds are not subject to many of the regulations that govern traditional investment vehicles, allowing them greater flexibility in investment strategies. Hedge funds often use leverage, derivatives, and other sophisticated techniques to seek high returns, often with higher risk levels. They may also employ hedging strategies to mitigate risk and protect capital in declining markets.

Home Health Care Rider: A home health care rider is an optional provision available with some insurance policies that provides coverage for home health care services. This rider typically covers expenses related to skilled nursing care, rehabilitative therapy, personal care assistance, and other services provided in the policyholder's home. It is designed to help policyholders maintain their independence and receive necessary care in the comfort of their own home.

House Money Effect: A behavioral finance concept that describes the tendency of individuals to take greater risks with money that they perceive as "won" or separate from their original capital. The term originated from the world of gambling, where players may become more willing to bet larger sums of money after experiencing a streak of wins, often feeling as though they are playing with "house money" rather than their own. In investing, the house money effect manifests when investors perceive gains in their portfolio as separate from their initial investment, leading them to take greater risks with those profits. This behavior can result in overconfidence and imprudent decision-making, such as increasing exposure to speculative investments or making larger bets than they normally would.

Immediate Annuity or Single Premium Immediate Annuity (SPIA): A type of annuity contract where an individual makes a lump-sum payment to an insurance company in exchange for a stream of income payments that begins immediately, usually within one year of the initial investment. The income payments from a SPIA are typically fixed and continue for the rest of the individual's life or for a specified period, such as a certain number of years. SPIAs can provide retirees with a steady and predictable income stream to supplement other sources of retirement income.

Index Fund: An index fund is a type of mutual fund or exchange-traded fund (ETF) that aims to replicate the performance of a specific market index, such as the S&P 500 or the Dow Jones Industrial Average. Instead of actively selecting individual stocks, index funds passively track the holdings of a particular index. They are known for their low costs and broad diversification; they generally aim to match the performance of the index they track rather than outperform it.

Interest Rates: Interest rates refer to the cost of borrowing money or the return on investment for lending money, expressed as a percentage. When you borrow money, such as through a loan or a mortgage, you typically pay interest to the lender as compensation for the use of their funds. On the other hand, when you deposit money in a savings account or invest in bonds, you earn interest on your investment. Interest rates are influenced by various factors, including central bank policies, inflation, economic growth, and market demand for credit. Central banks, such as the Federal Reserve in the United States, often set short-term interest rates as a means of controlling inflation and stimulating economic activity.

IRA (Individual Retirement Account): An individual retirement account is a tax-advantaged savings account designed to help individuals save for retirement. There are two main types of IRAs: traditional IRAs and Roth IRAs. With a traditional IRA, contributions may be tax-deductible, and investments grow tax-deferred until withdrawals are made in retirement, at which point they are taxed as ordinary income. With a Roth IRA, contributions are made with after-tax dollars, but qualified withdrawals in retirement are tax-free. IRAs offer a wide range of investment options, including stocks, bonds, mutual funds, and other assets.

Irrevocable Trust: An irrevocable trust is a type of trust that cannot be modified or revoked once it is established, except under very limited circumstances and with the consent of all beneficiaries. Once assets are transferred into an irrevocable trust, they are no longer considered part of the grantor's estate and are subject to the terms of the trust. Irrevocable trusts are commonly used for estate planning purposes to protect assets, minimize estate taxes, provide for beneficiaries, and plan for long-term care or special needs.

Life Insurance Retirement Plan (LIRP): A life insurance retirement plan, also known as an LIRP, is an advanced life insurance strategy that combines permanent life insurance with a cash value component that can be accessed in retirement as a source of tax-free income. Policyholders contribute premiums to the life insurance policy, which accumulates cash value over time. During retirement, policyholders can access the cash value through withdrawals or policy loans, which are generally not subject to income tax.

Long-Term Care: Long-term care refers to a range of services and support designed to help individuals with chronic illnesses, disabilities, or other conditions meet their daily health care needs over an extended period. Long-term care services may include assistance with activities of daily living (such as bathing, dressing, and eating), skilled nursing care, rehabilitative therapy, and custodial care provided in nursing homes, assisted living facilities, or at home.

Market-Based Portfolio: A market-based portfolio is an investment portfolio constructed primarily of securities that are bought and sold in financial markets, such as stocks, bonds, mutual funds, and exchange-traded funds (ETFs). The composition of a market-based portfolio may vary depending on an investor's financial goals, risk tolerance, investment horizon, and other factors. Market-based portfolios are typically designed to generate returns based on the performance of the underlying securities and market conditions. Investors may employ various investment strategies, such as asset allocation, diversification, and active or passive management, to build and manage a market-based portfolio that aligns with their investment objectives. Market-based portfolios are subject to market risk, including fluctuations in asset prices, interest rates, and economic conditions, and investors should carefully consider their risk tolerance and investment time horizon when constructing and managing such portfolios.

Medicaid: Medicaid is a joint federal and state government program that provides health insurance coverage to low-income individuals and families, including children, pregnant women, elderly adults, and people with disabilities. Medicaid covers a wide range of medical services, including doctor visits, hospital care, prescription drugs, and long-term care.

Medicare: Medicare is a federal government program that provides health insurance coverage to individuals aged sixty-five and older, as well as certain younger people with disabilities and individuals with end-stage renal disease. Medicare consists of several parts, including Part A (hospital insurance), Part B (medical insurance), Part C (Medicare Advantage plans), and Part D (prescription drug coverage).

Multi-Bagger: A term used to describe an investment that has gained several times its initial value, often referring to a stock that has appreciated significantly over time. For example, if an investor bought a stock at $10 per share and it later reached $100 per share, that stock would be considered a multi-bagger because it has increased by tenfold or more.

Mutual Fund: A mutual fund is a type of investment vehicle that pools money from multiple investors to invest in a diversified portfolio of securities, such as stocks, bonds, or a combination of both. The fund is managed by professional portfolio managers, who make investment decisions based on the fund's investment objectives and strategies. Investors in a mutual fund own shares of the fund, which represent a proportional ownership of the fund's assets. Mutual funds offer diversification, professional management, and liquidity, as investors can typically buy or sell shares of the fund at the end of each trading day at the net asset value (NAV) price.

Net Unrealized Appreciation (NUA): Net unrealized appreciation refers to the increase in the value of an employer-sponsored retirement plan's employer stock that has not yet been realized by selling the stock. NUA typically arises when an employee holds company stock within a qualified retirement plan, such as a 401(k), and the value of that stock increases over time. When the employee distributes the employer stock from the retirement plan, they are typically taxed only on the cost basis (the original purchase price) of the stock at ordinary income tax rates. The appreciation in the stock's value, known as the NUA, is taxed at long-term capital gains rates when the stock is eventually sold, potentially resulting in significant tax savings for the employee.

Ordinary Income: This is income earned from regular sources such as wages, salaries, commissions, tips, and interest from non-tax-advantaged accounts (banking, CDs, fixed income, etc.). Additionally, income from pensions, annuities, royalties, and rental properties is typically considered ordinary income unless specific tax treatment applies. Ordinary income is subject to taxation at the individual's applicable marginal tax rate, which may vary depending on the amount of income earned and the individual's tax filing status. In contrast, certain types of income, such as long-term capital gains and qualified dividends, are taxed at preferential rates separate from ordinary income tax rates.

Passive Management: Passive management, also known as passive investing or indexing, is an investment strategy that aims to replicate the performance of a specific market index, such as the S&P 500, rather than actively selecting individual securities in an attempt to outperform the market. Passive management typically involves investing in index funds or exchange-traded funds (ETFs) that hold all or a representative sample of the securities included in the target index. Passive management is known for its low costs, broad diversification, and adherence to a buy-and-hold investment approach.

Pension Protection Act of 2006: The Pension Protection Act of 2006 is a federal law enacted to strengthen and reform retirement plan rules and regulations. It includes provisions aimed at improving pension plan funding, increasing transparency and accountability in plan management, encouraging retirement savings, and expanding access to retirement plans for small businesses and employees.

Phantom Income: Phantom income refers to income that is reported for tax purposes but not actually received in cash by the taxpayer. This can occur in various situations, such as when an investor holds certain types of investments, like partnerships or real estate investment trusts (REITs), that pass through taxable income to investors even if no cash distributions are made. Phantom income can result in tax obligations for investors without corresponding cash flow to pay the taxes.

Private Equity: Private equity (PE) refers to investments made in privately held companies, often with the goal of acquiring a significant ownership stake or outright control of the company. PE firms raise capital from institutional investors and wealthy individuals and then use this capital to acquire, invest in, or provide financing for private companies. PE investments can take various forms, including leveraged buyouts, growth capital, and distressed debt investments. PE investors typically aim to improve the operational and financial performance of their portfolio companies and ultimately sell them for a profit, often through a merger, acquisition, or IPO.

Protective Put: A protective put is an options trading strategy used to protect against downside risk in an investment. In this strategy, an investor purchases put options on a security they already own (or intend to purchase). A put option gives the holder the right, but not the obligation, to sell the underlying asset at a predetermined price (strike price) within a specified period (until expiration). By purchasing put options, the investor can limit potential losses if the price of the underlying asset declines, as they have the right to sell the asset at the strike price, regardless of how far the price falls.

Qualified Charitable distributions (QCDs): Qualified charitable distributions are direct transfers of funds from an Individual Retirement Account (IRA) to eligible charitable organizations, typically done by individuals who are at least seventy and a half years old. These distributions are made directly to the charity and count toward the individual's required minimum distribution (RMD) for the year. QCDs are excluded from the individual's taxable income, providing a tax-efficient way to support charitable causes while fulfilling RMD requirements. The current limit is $105,000 per donor per year. For married couples, each spouse can make QCDs up to the $105,000 limit for a potential total of $210,000. To qualify, the charitable organization must be eligible to receive tax-deductible contributions, and certain limitations and requirements apply.

Qualified Dividends: Qualified dividends meet specific criteria set by the Internal Revenue Service (IRS) to qualify for lower tax rates. To be considered qualified, the dividends must be paid by a US corporation or a qualified foreign corporation, and the investor must meet certain holding period requirements. Typically, the holding period requires that the stock be held for more than sixty days during the 121-day period that begins sixty days before the ex-dividend date. Qualified dividends are taxed at long-term capital gains tax rates, which are typically lower than ordinary income tax rates.

Real Estate Investment Trust (REIT): A real estate investment trust is a company that owns, operates, or finances income-generating real estate across a range of property sectors, including residential, commercial, retail, and industrial properties. REITs allow individual investors to invest in a diversified portfolio of real estate assets without directly owning or managing the properties themselves. They are required by law to distribute a significant portion of their taxable income to shareholders in the form of dividends, making them attractive for income-oriented investors. REITs can be publicly traded on stock exchanges or privately held.

Recency Bias: Recency bias is a cognitive bias that leads individuals to give more weight or significance to recent events or experiences over older ones when making decisions or forming judgments. In the context of investing, recency bias causes investors to rely too heavily on recent market trends or performance data when making investment decisions, rather than considering the broader historical context or long-term fundamentals. For example, investors affected by recency bias may believe that a stock will continue to perform well simply because it has been rising in value recently, without considering factors such as valuation metrics, market conditions, or company fundamentals. Conversely, they may avoid investing in an asset that has experienced recent losses, assuming that the downward trend will continue indefinitely, despite potential opportunities for value or recovery.

Required Minimum Distribution (RMD): RMDs are the amount of money that retirement account owners, typically those with IRAs or employer-sponsored retirement plans like 401(k)s, must withdraw from their accounts each year once they reach a certain age, usually starting at age seventy-three. The purpose of RMDs is to ensure that individuals withdraw a portion of their retirement savings and pay taxes on that money as it has grown tax-deferred over the years.

Retirement Red Zone: The retirement red zone refers to the critical period in the years leading up to retirement when individuals are nearing their retirement age and need to make crucial financial decisions to ensure they are adequately prepared for retirement. This term is often used to describe the period roughly five to ten years before retirement, although the specific timeframe may vary depending on individual circumstances.

Risk Capacity: Risk capacity refers to the ability of an individual, organization, or investment portfolio to withstand potential financial losses without significantly impacting their financial well-being or ability to meet their financial goals. It is primarily influenced by objective financial factors such as income, assets, liabilities, time horizon, and overall financial stability. For example, a person with a stable income, substantial savings, and a long investment horizon typically has a higher risk capacity, as they can afford to take on more investment risk without jeopardizing their financial security. Financial advisors often assess clients' risk capacity to determine appropriate investment strategies that align with their financial circumstances and goals.

Risk Tolerance: Risk tolerance refers to an individual's psychological willingness or comfort level with taking on investment risk. It reflects an individual's attitudes, preferences, and emotions towards risk and can vary significantly from person to person. Risk tolerance is influenced by various factors, including temperament, past investment experiences, future expectations, and personal financial goals. Some investors may have a high risk tolerance and feel comfortable taking on significant investment risk in pursuit of higher returns, while others may have a low risk tolerance and prefer to prioritize capital preservation and stability over potential growth. Financial advisors often assess clients' risk tolerance through questionnaires or discussions to tailor investment recommendations that align with their comfort level and financial objectives.

Roth Conversion: A Roth conversion is the process of transferring funds from a traditional IRA or employer-sponsored retirement plan (such as a 401(k) or 403(b)) to a Roth IRA. This conversion results in taxable income in the year of the conversion, as the funds moved from the traditional account to the Roth account are treated as ordinary income. However, once the funds are in the Roth IRA, they can grow tax-free, and qualified withdrawals in retirement are tax-free as well.

Roth IRA: A Roth IRA is an individual retirement account that allows individuals to contribute after-tax income to the account, and withdrawals in retirement are generally tax-free, including both contributions and investment earnings, as long as certain conditions are met. Unlike traditional IRAs, contributions to a Roth IRA are not tax-deductible, but qualified distributions in retirement are tax-free. Roth IRAs offer flexibility, as contributions can be withdrawn at any time without penalty, although earnings may be subject to taxes and penalties if withdrawn before age fifty-nine and a half or before meeting other requirements.

Securities and Exchange Commission (SEC): The SEC is a federal regulatory agency in the United

States responsible for overseeing and enforcing securities laws, regulating the securities industry, and protecting investors. The SEC was established in 1934 through the Securities Exchange Act in response to the stock market crash of 1929 and the subsequent Great Depression. The mission of the SEC is to promote fair and efficient capital markets, facilitate capital formation, and protect investors from fraudulent or manipulative practices in the securities markets. The SEC achieves its objectives through various activities, including the registration and regulation of securities exchanges, securities brokers and dealers, investment advisors, and mutual funds; enforcement of securities laws and regulations; investigation of securities violations and fraud; and the provision of investor education and information. The SEC plays a crucial role in maintaining the integrity and transparency of the US securities markets and promoting investor confidence.

Social Security: Social Security is a federal government program established in 1935 to provide financial assistance to retired workers, disabled individuals, and their dependents. It is funded through payroll taxes collected from employees and employers and provides monthly benefits to eligible individuals based on their work history and earnings record.

Standard Deviation: Standard deviation is a statistical measure of the dispersion or variability of a set of values from their mean (average). It quantifies the extent to which individual data points in a data set differ from the mean, providing a measure of the average distance between each data point and the mean. A higher standard deviation indicates that the data points are more spread out or dispersed from the mean, while a lower standard deviation suggests that the data points are closer to the mean. Standard deviation is calculated by taking the square root of the variance, which is the average of the squared differences between each data point and the mean. It is widely used in various fields, including finance, economics, science, and engineering, to analyze and interpret the variability or volatility of data sets and to make informed decisions based on statistical significance.

Stocks: Stocks, also known as equities, represent ownership in a company. When you buy stock in a company, you essentially own a small piece of that company. Stockholders typically have voting rights in the company's decisions and may receive dividends if the company distributes profits. The value of stocks fluctuates based on factors like company performance, market conditions, and investor sentiment.

Tax Alpha: Tax alpha refers to the incremental after-tax returns generated by implementing tax-efficient investment strategies that minimize taxes and maximize after-tax investment returns. Tax alpha can be achieved through various tax-efficient investment strategies, such as tax-loss harvesting, asset location, and selecting

tax-advantaged investment vehicles. Maximizing tax
alpha can help investors improve their overall investment
performance and achieve their financial goals more
effectively.

Tax-Loss Harvesting: Tax-loss harvesting is an
investment strategy used to minimize taxes by selling
investments that have experienced losses and using those
losses to offset capital gains or ordinary income for tax
purposes. Investors can sell losing investments to realize
the losses, which can then be used to reduce taxable
income or offset gains from other investments. Tax-loss
harvesting can help investors reduce their tax liabilities
and improve after-tax investment returns.

Track Record Investing: Track record investing
refers to the practice of making investment decisions
based solely on the past performance of an investment,
without considering other factors such as market
conditions, economic fundamentals, or the specific
circumstances that contributed to past success. Investors
who engage in track record investing may be attracted to
investments or fund managers with impressive historical
returns, assuming that past performance is indicative of
future results. However, it's important to recognize that
past performance is not a guarantee of future success, and
relying solely on track records can lead to suboptimal
investment decisions.

Turnover Rate: Turnover rate, in investment terms, refers to the frequency with which securities within an investment portfolio are bought and sold over a specific period, typically one year. It is calculated by dividing the total value of securities bought or sold (whichever is less) by the average total value of the portfolio over the same period. A high turnover rate indicates that a significant portion of the portfolio's holdings has been replaced within the year, while a low turnover rate suggests that the portfolio has experienced minimal trading activity.

Umbrella Liability Coverage: Umbrella liability coverage is a type of insurance that provides additional liability protection beyond the limits of a primary insurance policy, such as auto or homeowners insurance. It acts as a "top-up" coverage, extending the coverage limits of the underlying policies in the event of a large liability claim or lawsuit. Umbrella liability coverage typically offers higher coverage limits than primary insurance policies, often starting at $1 million or more. It provides protection against various liability risks, including bodily injury, property damage, personal injury, and legal defense costs. For example, if someone is injured on your property and sues you for damages that exceed the liability limits of your homeowners insurance, umbrella liability coverage can help cover the additional costs, such as medical expenses, legal fees, and court judgments.

Variable Annuity: A variable annuity is a type of insurance product that provides investors with a tax-deferred investment vehicle designed to provide a stream of income in retirement. With a variable annuity, investors contribute premiums to the annuity contract, which are then invested in a selection of sub-accounts that function similarly to mutual funds and can invest in stocks, bonds, or other securities. The value of the annuity's underlying investments fluctuates based on market performance, and the annuity contract may offer a variety of optional features, such as death benefits, guaranteed minimum income benefits, or living benefit riders. Annuity payments can be structured as either a lump sum or a series of periodic payments, providing retirees with a source of income during their retirement years.

Venture Capital (VC): Venture capital refers to a type of private equity investment typically provided to early-stage, high-potential startup companies that have the potential for rapid growth. VC firms raise funds from institutional investors, high-net-worth individuals, and other sources, and then invest in startups in exchange for equity ownership. Venture capitalists often take an active role in guiding the growth and strategic direction of the companies they invest in, and they aim to realize significant returns when these companies are either acquired by larger firms or go public through an initial public offering (IPO).

Wash-Sale Rule: The wash-sale rule is a tax regulation that prohibits investors from claiming a tax deduction for a security sold in a wash sale. A wash sale occurs when an investor sells a security at a loss and then repurchases the same or a substantially identical security within thirty days before or after the sale. If a wash sale occurs, the IRS disallows the tax deduction for the loss, and the loss is added to the cost basis of the repurchased security.

About the Authors

Steven and Matthew Paul are co-hosts of the show *Retirement Approved*, which can be found on YouTube, Spotify, and Apple.

Matthew Paul, Chief Operating Officer at Richard Paul & Associates, brings a wealth of experience and knowledge to the table. As an Investment Advisory Representative and a Certified Financial Planner™ professional, Matthew oversees the day-to-day operations of the business with precision and dedication. He graduated from Michigan State University with a degree in economics and is licensed in life and health insurance. Matthew resides in Whitmore Lake with his wife Rachael and their daughter Ozzi. When he's not busy crunching numbers, Matthew enjoys cheering for Detroit sports teams, boating, and spending quality time with his family and friends.

Steven Paul, Senior Partner at Richard Paul & Associates, leads the financial planning team with expertise and finesse. Specializing in designing personalized retirement income plans, Steven is also a Certified Financial Planner™ professional who completed his education at Eastern Michigan University and Kaplan. With a bachelor's degree in economics from Wayne State University, Steven is well-equipped to navigate the intricacies of financial planning. He and his wife Michelle are proud parents to three lively children: Shay, Silas, and Seth. In his leisure time, Steven enjoys being outdoors, golfing, and all the wonderful things that come with being a father of three.